EARTHSHIPS

Building a zero carbon future for homes

The dream is this: envisage a building that is, without exaggeration, a passport to freedom, where it is not necessary to work to pay utility bills, because there are none. Your home effortlessly heats itself in winter and cools itself in summer, harvests water every time it rains and recycles that same water for multiple uses. Whenever the sun shines and the wind blows, electrical energy is pumped into your house and stored for your use.

The water recycling system allows for the cultivation of numerous edible plants within the building itself, and you are able to live happy in the knowledge that your footprint on the earth produces a negligible level of carbon emissions and uses only bountiful and renewable resources that are flowing freely from nature to sustain your life.

The building you live in looks after you and cares for your needs. Ecological living through earthships is not about privation but about an improvement of the quality of life for its inhabitants and their descendants.

EARTHSHIPS

Building a zero carbon future for homes

Mischa Hewitt and Kevin Telfer

Foreword by Kevin McCloud

bre press

Published by IHS BRE Press

Details of all publications from IHS BRE Press are
available from:
www.ihsbrepress.com
or
IHS BRE Press, Willoughby Road, Bracknell,
Berkshire RG12 8FB
Tel: 01344 328038
Fax: 01344 714440
Email: brepress@ihs.com

Printed on paper sourced from responsibly managed
forests

Cover image by Mischa Hewitt

Index compiled by Margaret Binns

Request to copy any part of this publication
should be made to:
IHS BRE Press, Garston, Watford WD25 9XX
Tel: 01923 664761 Email: brepress@ihs.com

EP 78

First published 2007

ISBN 978-1-86081-972-8

CONTENTS

Foreword   ix

Acknowledgements   xi

About the authors   xiii

Illustrations   xv

CHAPTER 1
INTRODUCTION
Background   1
Zero carbon homes as a government target   2
The effects of climate change   2
Origins of the earthship   8
Earthships in the UK   9
Summary of contents   11
References and notes   13

CHAPTER 2
WHAT IS AN EARTHSHIP?
Introduction   15
Low carbon living in luxury   16
Site harmony and synergy   16
Living within our means   18
Autonomy and self-sufficiency   18
The evolution of the earthship idea   19
Aesthetics and functionality   21
Modular design – different types of earthship   24
Elements of sustainable construction   24
Use of low impact materials in construction   25
Conclusion   28
References and notes   28

CHAPTER 3
THERMAL MASS
Introduction   31
Passive solar design in earthships   32
Thermal mass and thermal wrap in earthships   33

Super insulation in earthships   34
The Brighton Earthship: Evaluating the thermal performance   36
Conclusion   42
Acknowledgements   42
References and notes   42

CHAPTER 4
RENEWABLE ENERGY

Introduction   45
Offgrid construction   46
Low energy future – the contemporary UK situation   46
Large scale infrastructure and its carbon implications   49
Energy demand management in earthships   51
Harvesting passive solar energy   51
Microrenewable systems   52
Financial implications of offgrid living   55
Conclusion   57
References and notes   58

CHAPTER 5
WATER

Introduction   61
Large scale water distribution under pressure   61
Tapping alternative water resources   63
Earthship water systems   65
Conclusion   73
References and notes   74

CHAPTER 6
BUILDING WITH WASTE

Introduction   77
Why use tyres?   78
Legislative and regulatory position for building with tyres   82
Specific risk assessment concerns with tyres   85
Other rules about waste handling   85
Conclusion: the current regulatory position for tyres   85
Other low embodied energy materials   86
'Junk aesthetic'   88
Conclusion   88
References and notes   89

CHAPTER 7
CONSTRUCTION METHODS

Introduction   91
Site selection and ground preparation   91
Tyre walls – methodology   92

Suitability of tyres   95
Tyre sizing and alternative tyre techniques   95
Wall construction   96
Roof construction   96
Adobe abode – tyre rendering preparation and pack out   97
Floors and foundations   97
Timber frame construction and glazing   98
Water systems installation   99
Natural ventilation   99
Material specification   100
Bottle walls and glass bricks   100
Plan view and room specification   101
Earthship Brighton: timeline   103
References and notes   104

CHAPTER 8
WHAT IS THE FUTURE OF EARTHSHIPS?

Introduction   107
Earthships as provocative agents of change   107
Zero carbon homes   108
Site harmony and one planet living   108
Critique of infrastructure   108
Building with waste and low embodied energy materials   109
Demand reduction and renewable supply   109
Passive solar, thermal mass and thermal performance   109
Water harvesting and recycling   110
Home building in the UK – a revolution in zero carbon homes?   110
Earthships as a mass zero carbon housing solution   113
Future earthship construction – specific builds   114
Earthship self-builds   115
Retrofitting the existing building stock   116
Conclusion – towards 2016   116
References and notes   117

References and notes   119

Recommended reading   123

Index   125

FOREWORD
Kevin McCloud

We are constructing more and faster on this planet than ever before. The rate of growth in China and the Middle East is such that developments are measured in square kilometres rather than square metres. And to meet this insatiable appetite for building we are gobbling vast quantities of materials. At the time of writing in 2007, China is set to be the global largest national consumer of construction materials – consuming nearly half the world's production of cement by 2010. Meanwhile if you think the problem is too distant and global to be relevant, Spain holds an impressive record: the Spanish get through one metric tonne of cement per person per year equalling 42 million tonnes a year. Spain is the official international home of concrete. It is conceivable that Spanish mothers will soon be giving birth to concrete children; and that SEAT might decide to launch a new concrete car.

The first problem with this rate of consumption is the carbon burden it places on the planet – a tonne of cement will produce a tonne of CO_2 for example. The second problem is that we are using resources at such a rate that if every human consumed at the rate we do in Britain, we'd need three planets' worth of raw materials and resources to sustain us. I don't think there's a clearer or easier metaphor than that for what sustainability needs to answer.

In the UK our own volume housing is not only very poorly designed (the average design spend per new house is just £200) but also often badly built, insufficiently insulated and thermally leaky. It's a wonder that the UK's house building manufacturers – and let's face it, houses are just products to them – haven't gone the way of Britain's car manufacturers.

They might yet because the Japanese and Germans are already building factories in the UK to build their own far superior houses.

So what should we be expecting? Well our homes clearly need to be more than products bumped off a production line. And they should be more than shelters or parking spaces for our bodies. We ought to be expecting buildings which delight us and make us feel like happier, better human beings. Places that are light, warm and ventilated with high ceilings, a view to infinity (it isn't difficult to give everyone a view of the sky and stars) and flexible, spacious accommodation. Proper architecture that's designed around human beings, not the balance sheet.

But our homes need to do this in a way which minimises their impact on the environment and leaves a tiny carbon footprint: size 1 maybe. Or how about homes which are carbon-depleting and resource-enriching? In other words, houses which are so well built and efficient that they sell electricity back to the grid and are constructed from materials which would otherwise end up in a landfill. Now we're talking.

Of course not every building in the land is going to be built out of recycled lager cans and concrete made from disposable nappies. That would make for a very strange and dull world. Indeed, what makes buildings and places exciting is diversity: the mix of textures, grain and richness that human beings revel in. And frankly, the vast majority of us want to live in a normal-looking house with walls we can wallpaper and somewhere to park the infotainment system. I know I do. So should every home be an Earthship? Of course not.

But should we have more of them? Oh yes we should. There is always room for the exemplary, the innovative and the experimental. I use these words carefully because they have a specific relationship to each other. Think of excellence as a triangle or pyramid divided into four strata. Wallowing at the bottom is a huge quantity of the mundane and mediocre, the everyday that we all have to put up with. In the case of our topic of conversation, that means noddy houses.

Above them lies a layer of exemplary projects: houses and schemes that offer a decent architectural experience with features like some extra light and space and headroom and something about the design which you can admire and enjoy. We're not talking Pritzker-Prize winning stuff, just nice well-built, well-insulated and sustainable homes. You may have difficulty understanding the type of building I'm talking about here and that's sadly because you won't have seen many. But there are more and more exemplary projects out there, like the work that Urban Splash or First Base do. Or that Peabody or Rowntree Trusts do. Or that many housing associations do.

An even smaller stratum comprises a tiny number of vanguard buildings and developments that are innovative. Innovative means that they take existing proven technologies and ideas and put them together in a commercial way. Think of Bill Dunster's BedZED scheme in Beddington, South London or the European Passivhaus model, which delivers houses that are airtight and superinsulated and fitted with heat-recovery systems, not boilers. There are now 4000 of these homes, which hardly makes them experimental.

But that's not to discount the experimental. Experimental design sits at the very dizzying pinnacle of our triangle. It comprises extreme student projects and real homes, often built as one-offs in which owners, usually at their own expense (bless them) devise and use new technologies and ideas into one project.

I have made a living filming and writing about experimental projects so I understand their value. Without the creativity of the brave humans who turn their lives into a living laboratory we would have nothing experimental to learn from and consequently nothing that was innovative or exemplary. Sadly we have so little of all of these categories that you wouldn't notice their absence driving around the country. There would still be the same sea of mediocrity.

But experimental projects are essential. The rest of the triangle feeds off the crackling brilliance of edgy invention. Sustainable development would not be possible on a large scale if there were no straw bale houses, no cob construction and no Superadobe Earthships.

So I salute this survey of the experimental and the innovative, of 'first adopters' and adventurers who inform the wider world with their exploits. They are the heroes of the construction world and this book is a fitting tribute.

Kevin McCloud, August 2007

ACKNOWLEDGEMENTS

Mike Reynolds deserves a special mention and he has been invaluable in providing insights into earthships in general and being a truly inspiring force. We would also like to thank Mike's longstanding associate Kirsten Jacobsen for her help and photographs.

Major thanks are due to Kevin McCloud for agreeing to write the foreword for this book as well as Jane Turnbull and Gina Pelham for their help in organising this.

Taus Larsen, Daren Howarth, Ollie Hodge of Open Eye Media, Charlotte MacPherson, Nick White of the Hockerton Housing Project, the Health Protection Agency, Darren Cool of Southern News and Pictures and Jo D'Ambra for their kind permission to reproduce their photographs and diagrams in this book. Ollie Mouland for the CAD drawings. Howard John's of Southern Solar for the use of the renewable power system sizing chart for Earthship Brighton.

We would like to thank Jon Priddey for his invaluable help both to the authors and to the Earthship Brighton project on the legislative and regulatory framework surrounding building with tyres and his ongoing work in this field.

Paula Cowie and Esmond Tressider of Sustainable Communities Initiative for background detail and photographs of the Earthship Fife project.

We would also like to thank Nick Clarke for his eminently sensible and consistently encouraging stance throughout the book writing project.

Mischa Hewitt – acknowledgements

All the members past and present of the Low Carbon Trust who have worked on the Earthship Brighton project over the years. Particularly, in no specific order: George Clinton, Bryn Thomas, Matt Bulba, Taus Larsen, Jon Kalviac, Ben East, Duncan Passmore, Mark Whittaker, Steve Bright, Alun Hughes, Jon Priddey, Jane Glenzinska, Owen Davies, Alexa King, Amanda King, Cheryl Broughton, Sarah Steer, Howard Johns, Andy Francis, Don MacLean, Daren Howarth and Gabrielle Saunders to name but a few.

Mike Reynolds and all the crew of Earthship Biotecture who have worked on the project at various times, particularly, Justin Simpson, Kirsten Jacobsen and Ron Sciarrillo who were there for the last charge.

The hundreds of volunteers over the last few years who have contributed their time and energy to the construction of the Earthship Brighton project and the landscaping of the surrounding grounds.

All the funders and other benevolent folk who helped make the Earthship Brighton project possible, including Peter Jones of Biffaward, Barry Beecroft of the BOC Foundation, Simon Wallwork of British Gas Business, Jonathon Best of Brighton and Hove Council, Nigel French and Andy Came of EDF Energy, Polly McLean, Corin Stewart, Dr Nick Banks for all his successful fundraising efforts for the renewable energy systems and Graham Hole for his financial wizardry.

All of the companies that donated materials and services to the project including Tom Bedford of BEP Consulting Engineers, Paul Hanratty of CA Group, Tony Mellon of Flag UK, Terry Payne of Monodraught,

Chris Brewster of Polypipe Civils, Craig Bligh of Rockwool, Susan Fitzpatrick of Saint-Gobain Glass, Mike Lief of Ubbink, Steve Osborne of David Cover & Sons, Andy Francis and Philip Naylor of RH Partnerships, John Packer of John Packer Associates, Iain Wilkinson of Wilkinson Waste & Waste Water Specialists.

John Harrison of TecEco for all the help and support needed to successfully mix and pour all the eco-cement slabs throughout Earthship Brighton.

Professor Andrew Miller and Kath Shaw of the University of Brighton for setting up the three-year thermographic study of Earthship Brighton performance and their ongoing work in the field as summarised in the thermal mass chapter.

Gareth Taylor of Cellecta for help with some of the U value calculations.

Tim Wraight for getting the idea of this book planted.

And finally my beautiful girlfriend Jo who has tolerated all the long hours and supported me throughout the Earthship Brighton project and the writing of this book.

Kevin Telfer – acknowledgements

I would like to thank my wife, Bridget, for her steadfast support throughout the writing of this book.

Other people and organisations that have helped, either directly or indirectly, and who I would like to thank are:

Taus Larsen, Jon Priddey, Ruth Slavid, Paul Finch, Keith Hall, Lin, Pete and Amy Ritchie and the Energy Institute.

ABOUT THE AUTHORS

MISCHA HEWITT is the project manager of the Earthship Brighton project, director of the Low Carbon Trust (www.lowcarbon.co.uk), and director of a green building specialist company Earthwise Construction (www.earthwiseconstruction.org), and is also involved in various other environmental projects.

KEVIN TELFER is a freelance journalist and author. He is the author, with Kevin McCloud, of the book *Grand Designs Abroad* that accompanied the Channel 4 TV series and has written for the *Architects' Journal*, *Building for a Future* magazine, *Grand Designs* magazine, *The Guardian* and *The Sunday Times*. He has also written a book about the history of Great Ormond Street Hospital for Children *The remarkable story of Great Ormond Street Hospital* – for more information see www.kevintelfer.com.

ILLUSTRATIONS

We express our thanks to the following for permission to use their illustrations in this book.

© **Chemical Hazards and Poisons Division (London) Health Protection Agency, 2003**
Page 77: A disused quarry – the Hampole tyre dump, near Doncaster

Darren Cool
Page 108: David Miliband, as the then secretary of state for the environment, visited Earthship Brighton in 2006, pictured with Mischa Hewitt

Jo D'Ambra
Page 76: Earthships show how materials such as tyres, which are usually considerered to be waste, can be used as effective building materials

Department of Communities and Local Government
Page 115: SAP ratings for dwellings from pre-1919 to post-1990 (based on the English House Condition Survey, 2004)

Energywatch
Page 3: Electricity and gas price comparisons over a 3-year period

Mischa Hewitt
Page 14: Earthship Brighton from the west

Page 18: View through bathroom wall (Earthship Brighton)

Page 35: Thermographic images of Earthship Brighton taken during the day

Page 45: Earthship Brighton showing a wind turbine, photovoltaic cells and solar thermal panels

Page 49: Trojan batteries before installation (Earthship Brighton)

Page 52: Whisper wind turbine (Earthship Brighton)

Page 53: Filsol solar thermal panels (Earthship Brighton)

Page 54: Photovoltaic panels at the Eden Project

Page 54: Filsol solar thermal panel and Unisolar photovoltaic panels (Earthship Brighton)

Page 55: Extraflame wood pellet stove (Earthship Brighton)

Page 57: A power organising module: controller, inverter and fusebox (Earthship Brighton)

Page 60: Rainwater harvesting system in action at the Eden Project's 'core' building

Page 69: Water organising module (Earthship Brighton)

Page 70: Rock bulb installation during greywater construction (Earthship Brighton)

Page 70: Plan view of greywater sump and rock bulbs during construction (Earthship Brighton)

Page 71: Filling a greywater planter with 10 mm gravel (Earthship Brighton)

Page 71: Sand raked in a greywater planter (Earthship Brighton)

Page 71: Raking gravel flat in a greywater planter (Earthship Brighton)

Page 72: Septic tank installation (Earthship Brighton)

Page 79: Exposed wall section (Earthship Brighton)

Page 85: Volunteer cutting glass bottles with a wet tile cutter (Earthship Brighton)

Page 86: Glass bottle brick wall (Earthship Brighton)

Page 86: Glass bottle brick wall showing 'porcupining' (Earthship Brighton)

Page 86: Close up of a glass bottle brick wall during construction (Earthship Brighton)

Page 86: Finished glass bottle brick wall with render (Earthship Brighton)

Page 87: Conservatory floor at Earthship Brighton made from reclaimed granite and marble off-cuts

Page 90: Earthship Brighton sunspace; floor and greywater planter wall made from reclaimed granite and adobe walls

Page 100: Gravity-fed skylight locked shut with clam cleat (Earthship Brighton)

Page 100: Open skylights (Earthship Brighton)

Page 102: Meeting room (Earthship Brighton)

Hockerton Housing Project

Page 44: Photovoltaic cells at the Hockerton Housing Project

Page 65: Hockerton Housing Project blackwater treatment lake

Oli Hodge (Open Eye Media)

Page 91: Site excavation and preparation for Earthship Brighton

Daniel Holloway

Page 53: Installing the whisper wind turbine (Earthship Brighton)

Daren Howarth

Page 67: Rain storage tanks before burial (Earthship Brighton)

Page 80: Tyre pounding in action (Taos, New Mexico)

Kirsten Jacobsen

Page 1: Hybrid earthship hut at night (Taos, New Mexico)

Page 4: Hut house kitchen (Taos, New Mexico)

Page 5: Reusing bottles in walls can create a beautiful visual effect (Taos, New Mexico)

Page 9: Kitchen area in the Estrada earthship (Taos, New Mexico)

Page 10: Jacobsen earthship at dusk (Taos, New Mexico)

Page 15: Hybrid earthship at night (Taos, New Mexico)

Page 17: Split level earthship (Taos, New Mexico)

Page 22: Staircase in the Estrada earthship (Taos, New Mexico)

Page 23: Mike Reynolds

Page 24: Adobe arches in the Kurnizi earthship (Taos, New Mexico)

Page 83: Interior view of glass bottle brick bathroom wall at the Jacobsen earthship (Taos, New Mexico)

Page 87: Exterior view of glass bottle brick bathroom at the Jacobsen earthship (Taos, New Mexico)

Page 106: Rear entrance to the Happy Castle at night (Taos, New Mexico)

Taus Larsen

Page 26: Hut wall construction (Earthship Brighton)

Page 32: Thermal wrap installation (Earthship Brighton)

Page 33: Solar gain section (Earthship Brighton)

Page 33: Limiting solar gain in summer (Earthship Brighton)

Page 33: Release of heat from thermal mass (Earthship Brighton)

Page 33: Convection through Earthship Brighton

Page 34: Installation of Rockwell Hardrock insulation (Earthship Brighton)

Page 67: Diagram of Earthship Brighton roof harvesting rain

Page 67: Rain storage tanks before burial (Earthship Brighton)

Page 67: Rain storage tanks after burial, and roof (Earthship Brighton)

Page 78: Rammed tyre walls (Earthship Fife)

Page 78: Rammed tyre walls (Earthship Brighton)

Page 81: Section of Earthship Brighton showing rammed tyre wall at rear and footing at the front

Page 93: Tyre store (Earthship Brighton)

Page 93: First course of tyres being laid on a damp proof course (Earthship Brighton)

Page 93: Filling first course of tyres with sand to protect the damp proof course (Earthship Brighton)

Page 94: Working on the seventh nest tyre wall (Earthship Brighton)

Page 94: Installation of battery box thermal wrap insulation (Earthship Brighton)

Page 94: Building the tyre walls of the hut module (Earthship Brighton)

Page 97: Attaching timber roof structure to wall plate and rammed tyre wall (Earthship Brighton)

Page 98: Pouring eco-cement floor slab (Earthship Brighton)

Page 98: Attaching the nest wall plate to rammed tyres (Earthship Brighton)

Page 98: Sloped front face timber wall plate (Earthship Brighton)

Page 98: Conservatory timber frame under construction (Earthship Brighton)

Page 98: Vertical timber face construction (Earthship Brighton)

Page 99: Roof structure (Earthship Brighton)

Page 99: Preliminary greywater planter wall preparation (Earthship Brighton)

Charlotte MacPherson
Page 30: Earthship Brighton under construction, glazing recently installed and footing built from recycled glass bottles

Met Office
Page 61: UK average annual rainfall distribution. (Crown Copyright 2007)

Ofwat
Page 62: Daily water loss through pipe leakage

Sustainable Communities Initiatives
Page 28: Greywater planter (Earthship Fife)

Page 55: Turgo Runner Stream Engine microhydro turbine (Earthship Fife)

Page 84: Aluminium can wall (Earthship Fife)

Page 97: Rammed tyre wall packout (Earthship Fife)

Page 104: Earthship Fife visitor centre opening

Kevin Telfer
Page 20: Earthship Fife visitor centre (Kinghorn, Scotland)

Page 27: Blackwater treatment (Earthship Fife)

Page 47: BedZED uses a combined heat and power plant and photovoltaic cells

Page 71: Fully planted greywater planter (Earthship Fife)

Page 72: Greywater feed pipe for toilet and pump panel (Earthship Brighton)

Page 74: Blackwater treatment system (Earthship Fife)

Page 111: BowZED in the east end of London is an exemplar of passive solar, passive ventilation and microgenerative residential design on a tightly constricted urban site. Could this be the future of zero carbon building in the UK?

Evan Tuer

Page 101: Earthsip Fife visitor centre opening

Waterwise
Page 63: Average domestic daily water consumption and use

CHAPTER 1
INTRODUCTION

BACKGROUND

Earthships are not whacky, 'way-out' or extremist buildings from the lunatic fringe. They should not be regarded as the domain of hippies, sock and sandal-wearing folk, assorted eco-nuts and survivalists. This book looks at what earthships are, rather than what they are not. In brief, earthships are a serious, rational and well designed architectural response to some of the challenges that face humankind in the 21st Century. They are also visually arresting, charismatic and extremely comfortable for those who live in them; indeed, they are often described as low carbon living in luxury. Not only do earthships address the fundamental question of how to provide safe shelter for their inhabitants, they have a thorough and holistic engagement with vital issues of sustainability, notably zero carbon and zero waste living, through recycling and reusing waste, energy saving and generation, water harvesting and recycling, and even food production.

During the course of writing this book, the agenda surrounding sustainable architectural practice in the UK has moved on so enormously as to necessitate numerous revisions to keep pace with the many

Figure 1: Hybrid earthship hut at night (Taos, New Mexico)

developments. In terms of the need for action to reduce carbon emissions, arguably the most notable of these is Sir Nicholas Stern's review on the economics of climate change published in October 2006.[1.1] Nicholas Stern states that there is a pressing economic need to find global solutions to climate change – potentially the greatest and widest ranging market failure the world has ever seen, which could, he argues, shrink the global economy by a fifth. He concludes that there is an absolute imperative to make significant reductions in manmade carbon production.

ZERO CARBON HOMES AS A GOVERNMENT TARGET

Zero carbon buildings, such as earthships, enable us to see how this reduction might take place: it is this, as much as anything else, which makes the earthship an essential building for study. The UK government target, that zero carbon homes will be the standard by 2016, was announced jointly in December 2006 by chancellor Gordon Brown, minister for communities Ruth Kelly, and minister for housing and planning Yvette Cooper, at the time of the launch of the Code for Sustainable Homes Initiative. Upon the launch of this Code – which replaces the BRE Environmental Assessment Method (BREEAM) EcoHomes standard – the Department for Communities and Local Government (DCLG) stated that "climate change is a real and imminent threat. The recent Stern Review brought into sharp relief the need for urgent international action. With a rising population and more people living in smaller households the demands on housing are set to increase. So it is vital that homes and other buildings are as sustainable and eco-friendly as possible. Further tough action is still needed to deliver significant energy use reductions in existing homes, but within a decade [we] want every new home to be zero carbon".[1.2] This aspiration in itself confirms that buildings such as earthships, far from being on the fringe of architecture, will be at the very core of the future of building not just in the UK, but globally.

The Code sits alongside the Energy Performance of Buildings Directive (2002), which came into force in January 2006. In accordance with the Directive all domestic and non-domestic buildings will be required to have an Energy Performance Certificate at some point during 2007.[1.3] This certificate will summarise the energy efficiency and carbon emissions from the home: for the first time at-a-glance information about a home's actual energy and carbon credentials will be available.

THE EFFECTS OF CLIMATE CHANGE

In July 2006, the hottest month since records began, the UK was gripped by a heat wave.[1.4] Europe and the USA were afflicted by the same phenomenon which was widely perceived as further evidence of global warming due to manmade carbon emissions. At the same time as the searing temperatures, power cuts took place in California and London as energy suppliers failed to meet the demand from air conditioning and refrigeration units. In south east England drought orders had been in place for a number of months, restricting water usage. In the same month British Gas announced price rises of 12% for their customers, and by October 2006 gas prices in the UK had, on average, increased by 91% against January 2003 prices, and electricity prices by 58% over the same period (Figure 2 and Box 1).[1.5]

All of this might not seem too directly relevant to architecture, but, of course, it is. On the most basic level, architecture should be providing safe shelter and a comfortable environment for its inhabitants. This includes provision of basic services essential to life such as water and temperature control – both cooling in hot weather and warming in cold weather. As soon as those basic functions are threatened, and are not being supplied by our buildings, then architecture is in danger of failing in the most fundamental sense.

This is the reality of the contemporary situation in the UK. In the grip of a heatwave people either have to suffer the stifling temperatures or rely on energy-hungry air conditioning, a solution that is financially expensive, ecologically harmful in terms of carbon emissions, and always in danger of failing – as happened in London and California in 2006 – due to the limitations of resources and infrastructure. To keep buildings warm in harsh winters people have to spend large amounts of money to pay utility companies that are charging more and more for the gas and electricity they supply – something that is beyond the means of an increasing number of people. The price of water is also rising above inflation and the surety of supply potentially in danger in some areas; this is due to a number of different reasons including population density in the south east of England, relatively high usage rates, wasteful behaviour and leakage through poor infrastructure.

In essence, the most basic functions of our buildings are at risk due to their reliance on weak centralised systems ie services provided by large scale infrastructure. Paul Hyett, a former Royal Institute of British Architects (RIBA) president, has argued

that we have "an architecture that is increasingly incapable of serving its most primitive purpose: providing safe shelter. Our modern cities continue to be torn apart to accommodate ecologically destructive buildings that have insatiable energy demands for even the most basic functions of ventilation, lighting and cooling".[1.6]

And it is arguably here that a great deal of modern architecture in general, both in the UK and much of the developing world, is going wrong as many architects fail to engage with the magnitude of their buildings' impact on the environment; in terms of

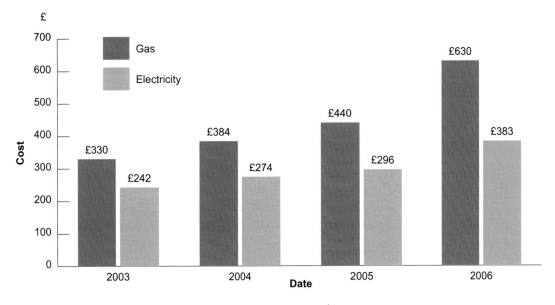

Figure 2: Electricity and gas price comparisons over a 3-year period

Box 1

Supplier	Gas			Electricity		
	January 03	October 06	Price rise	January 03	October 06	Price rise
British Gas	£370	£707	91%	£237	£428	81%
EDF	£324	£641	98%	£240	£357	49%
Npower	£329	£628	91%	£234	£400	71%
Powergen	£311	£644	107%	£241	£392	63%
Scottish Power	£319	£622	95%	£251	£379	51%
Scottish and Southern Energy	£326	541%*	66%*	£246	£342*	39%*
Across UK	£330	£630	91%	£242	£383	58%

* Does not include recently announced rises which came into effect in January 2007.

Based on an average annual gas consumption of 20 500 kWh and an average annual electricity consumption of 3300 kWh, paying by quarterly standard credit. Figures from Energywatch price comparison fact sheets.

Figure 3: Hut house kitchen (Taos, New Mexico)

the resources that are used to construct buildings, the immediate environment in which a building is situated and the energy needs for space heating, ventilation and lighting that form such a large part of a building's carbon footprint. Of course architects alone are not always to blame – the clients who commission them are often unsympathetic to a sustainable agenda, particularly with the capital cost implications involved, and there are also significant cultural and legislative hurdles in place. But architects are also design leaders and it is surely their particular challenge to, at the very least, fulfil Paul Hyett's definition of the most fundamental goal in architecture – providing safe shelter fit for comfortable human habitation.

This is even more the case when we consider how nature can still have such a profound and potentially destructive impact on people and structures despite the apparent reassurance of modern technology. Technology is the tool with which mankind has tried to 'tame' nature and yet globally, people remain vulnerable in the face of extreme weather conditions and natural disaster – including tsunamis, earthquakes, volcanic eruption, flooding, storms and

avalanche. The Indian Ocean tsunami of December 2004 was one of the worst natural disasters in human history claiming more than 200 000 lives.[1.7] 2005 saw the devastation of a city – New Orleans – in the world's richest nation. These events underline the fact that human society exists within nature; buildings and cities sit upon the earth and no matter what the wealth of a nation, nature is capable of wreaking chaos on an apocalyptic scale. Yet the delusion persists that man has somehow achieved dominance over the earth; and the majority of modern buildings reflect just such a delusion.

The extent to which architecture can help in protecting people from disasters of the magnitude of the Asian tsunami and the New Orleans hurricane, and subsequent flooding, is debatable. But the types of building that people live in could certainly have had a massive impact on another recent natural disaster that unfolded over a number of weeks in 2003 when thousands of people throughout Europe perished in a heat wave. The *New Scientist* reported that there were 35 000 deaths in Europe from the 2003 heat wave with almost 15 000 of those in France alone and more than 2000 in the UK.[1.8] That extraordinary statistic, though, masks the fact that climate related deaths are actually commonplace in the UK with at least 25 000 people dying every winter from the cold, largely due to a combination of inadequate insulation and fuel poverty.[1.9]

Both these phenomena rank as large scale natural disasters with great loss of life and point to the fact that buildings have not been effective in protecting people from the extremes of nature. But not only have buildings failed to protect people, the way they are designed has actually increased people's vulnerability to the capriciousness of the elements due to the fact that their basic structure needs such fundamental support from other systems and finite resources to fulfil their core functions. That might be acceptable if those systems were reliable, clean and inexpensive, but they are none of these. And that is why design solutions to these problems need to be found – why should homeowners have to cover the overheads because their buildings are so fundamentally inefficient? And why should the environment always be the net loser in this

equation? Architects have always been at the forefront of innovation and change; arguably their greatest design challenge now is to respond to the lessons that nature has taught mankind, and build a sustainable future for a new millennium.

It now seems inevitable, even if carbon dioxide and other greenhouse gas emissions are effectively controlled and cut back significantly, that climate change will teach mankind many more such lessons in the future as the world slowly heats up. The consequences of this change are so profound and potentially catastrophic on a global scale as to lead environmentalist, author and journalist George Monbiot to comment that "one of the problems with climate change is that it stretches the imagination to breaking point".[1.10] The Royal Society, one of the world's leading scientific organisations, states that the "possible consequences of climate change include rising temperatures, changing sea levels, and impacts on global weather. These changes could have serious impacts on the world's organisms and on the lives of millions of people, especially those living in areas

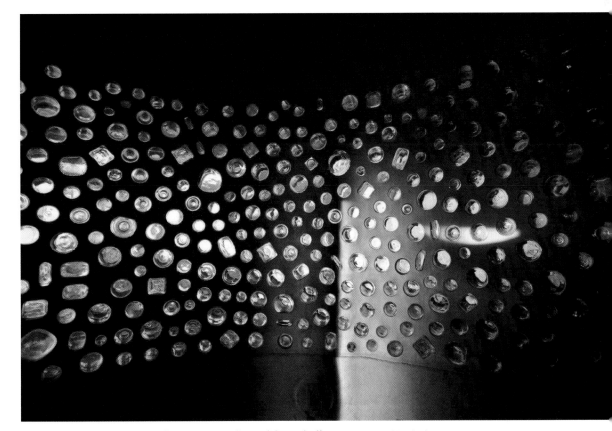

Figure 4: Reusing bottles in walls can create a beautiful visual effect (Taos, New Mexico)

Box 2

CLIMATE CHANGE – THE DEBATE IS OVER

Introduction to the Intergovernmental Panel on Climate Change's Fourth Assessment Report

Over the last couple of decades the phenomena of global warming or climate change, its origins, causes and severity has been widely criticised by some as having little or no real scientific basis in fact. The Fourth Assessment Report of the Intergovernmental Panel on Climate Change (IPCC) was released in February 2007. This IPCC was formed in 1988 as an independent organisation that could provide objective accurate scientific advice about all aspects of climate change. The report is not specifically new research but a thorough up-to-date stocktake of all collated data, information and climatic studies. It has been compiled from the work of over 2500 scientists and over 130 countries have contributed to the process. The report is more vigorous and confident than its three predecessors as the observable impacts of the climate change we are already experiencing become more apparent. The IPCC report states unequivocally that there is "at least a nine out of 10 chance" the increase in carbon dioxide levels have been caused by and continue to be caused by the sum of all human activities. The report is the first of three to be published in 2007; the others will focus on the impacts of climate change and actions needed to mitigate the problem.

Carbon dioxide and other greenhouse gas levels

There are a basket of greenhouse gases, but the main one is carbon dioxide, now at the highest level for over half a million years. Concentrations in the atmosphere stood at 379 parts per million (ppm) in 2005, compared to 278 ppm in pre-industrial times and outside of the natural range of 180 to 300 ppm over the last 650 000 years. A more potent but less produced greenhouse gas, methane, is now also far outside of the 'natural' range of atmospheric concentration, standing at 1774 parts per billion (ppb) in 2005, comparing to 715 ppb in pre-industrial times before 1750. The main reasons for the release of vast amounts of carbon dioxide are from the consumption of fossil fuel and land use. Whilst the average rate of increase in carbon dioxide emissions has been fairly constant at around 1.4 ppm per year since 1965, the figures from 1995 to 2005 show an alarming increase to 1.9 ppm per year demonstrating acceleration in the trend of carbon dioxide release into the atmosphere.

Global temperature rise

Higher increase in carbon dioxide concentration in the atmosphere brings higher average global temperature. The average temperature has already risen by 0.7°C in the last 100 years, with 11 of the 12 hottest years on record occurring between 1995 and 2006. The report states that over the next couple of decades we are already committed to a 0.2°C rise per decade, indeed we can

expect 0.6°C increase in the future whatever we do. The temperature increase we can expect to see before 2100 varies considerably depending on population levels and the level of use of fossil fuel in industrial activities, power stations, in homes and cars. The best estimate is that the average global temperature will rise between 1.8°C to 4°C over the next century, although in the temperature climates of the higher latitudes such as the UK it will be higher. An even more extreme rise of 6.4°C has been predicted if a business as usual model of unchecked economic growth with continuing high levels of fossil fuel consumption is pursued. It is worth noting that this not science fiction; all the climate change scenarios presented in the report have been peer reviewed by over 600 meteorologists. A rise of just 3°C would have catastrophic results on weather patterns, agriculture and ultimately human civilization.

Feedbacks and the earth's ability to cope

As the earth's temperature rises, its ability to absorb carbon dioxide through natural mechanisms such as the oceans and trees becomes increasingly strained. It is estimated that around half of the carbon dioxide that has been released by human activity so far has been absorbed by these natural carbon sinks, but this is not without consequence. It has been measured that carbon dioxide absorbed by the oceans is slowly acidifying them as the chemical reaction creates carbolic acid. This continuing process makes it increasingly difficult for marine animals that require an alkali environment to form their shells to survive. These animals often form the basis of the oceans food chain. Ultimately all carbon dioxide not absorbed by these natural processes remains in the atmosphere further exasperating the greenhouse effect and adding to global temperature increase.

Conclusion

The IPCC's fourth report is disturbing reading that demonstrates that the planet we live on is becoming increasingly stressed with our fossil fuel based lifestyles. Not only that but as time goes by the ability of the earth to shrug off the impacts of our carbon intensive lifestyle becomes impaired as temperatures rise. There has been an observed 0.74°C rise in the global average temperature over the last century and the link between this, human activity, fossil fuel use and carbon dioxide emissions has been established without the shadow of a doubt.

Each year that passes is one more year where inaction has further increased the problem and the concentration of carbon dioxide in the atmosphere. If we look back into the dark mists of time we can see an earth that had an average temperature very similar to the level that we are beginning to push towards. That world is very distant and very different and not one we would be very comfortable with, if indeed we would have any significant place at all.

vulnerable to extreme natural conditions such as flooding and drought".[1.11] With more unpredictable patterns of weather where heat wave, drought and floods are likely to become increasingly common, it is essential that thought is put into how buildings are going to cope with these severe conditions. But it is equally essential that there is a dramatic reduction in the amount of carbon being put into the earth's atmosphere in order to try and limit the amount of damage done by climate change. Currently, the energy used to heat, light and run our homes accounts for 27% of all of the UK's carbon emissions – around 40 million tonnes.[1.12] The adequacy of the government's proposed response needs to be seen in actions – in this case large numbers of zero carbon homes actually being built – rather than words, but the noises, at least, are encouraging.

And yet it does not need to be this way. Earthships offer solutions to both of the most pertinent problems regarding climate change: reducing the amount of building related carbon emissions without compromising comfort and ensuring that building services can still function in extreme conditions in which large scale infrastructure may be disrupted (often rather clumsily called 'passive survivability').

ORIGINS OF THE EARTHSHIP

The original inspiration for designing earthships came from news stories. Mike Reynolds, the American architect who invented the earthship concept, said that he was 'basically responding to the news' when he had the idea to design a radically new type of structure.[1.13] The news in the early 1970s told him there were huge environmental problems being faced along with a 'major energy crunch'.[1.13] His solution was to design a building made largely from waste materials – principally old car tyres – that aimed to take full advantage of natural resources: earth, sun, wind and rain. He chose a highly challenging environment in which to do this – the high mountain desert of Taos county in New Mexico, about 2000 m (7000 ft) above sea level with extremes of temperature varying between 40°C (104°F) in the summer and -10°C (14°F) in the winter, and with an annual precipitation of only approximately 300 mm (compared to approximately 550 to 700 mm in London, for example).[1.14] The earthships have evolved from being a specific design

solution to a particular set of climatic conditions in the New Mexican desert, to a paradigm that has been adapted to different climates across the planet. And that includes here, in the UK. At the time of writing there are two fully functioning earthships in the UK, in Kinghorn Loch, Fife, and Brighton, East Sussex: both non-residential demonstration 'prototypes' that were developed between 2000 and 2006. However, a significant development of between nine and 16 earthships (also in Brighton) built for residential use has been proposed and planning permission is being sought.

The earthship that has evolved over 30 years of trial and error in the unforgiving environment of New Mexico is a totally offgrid construction, unconnected to electricity, gas, water mains or sewage systems. In essence it has to look after itself out there in the big bad desert. And it does it remarkably well, anecdotally maintaining an interior ambient temperature throughout all seasons (and without any kind of electrical air conditioning system) of between 18°C and 23°C. Mike Reynolds, on a visit to the UK in 2006, told a story about some visitors he had taken to one of his earthships. "I took some people from Colorado into this room last week and it was 100°F (38°C) outside and they were sweltering getting out of their cars to walk to the building and in the room they thought we had an air conditioning system. When they found out we didn't, they wanted an earthship!"[1.15]

Sustainable space heating and passive ventilation, impressive as they are, are not the only admirable features of earthships. And this is a significant point – earthships offer a holistic version of sustainability rather than just a zero carbon footprint. The building also harvests its own water, which is then recycled to make it fulfil as many uses as possible, and generates its own electricity from microrenewable sources. The greywater planters that form the basis of the water recycling process also offer the opportunity to grow food, including bananas, grapes, tomatoes and herbs – even in the harsh winters of New Mexico. In essence, then, the earthship is an almost wholly autonomous, self-reliant building that uses waste materials in its construction and has a zero carbon footprint in its day-to-day running. After construction it is also extremely cheap to run with no utility bills to pay at all.

Figure 5: Kitchen area in the Estrada earthship (Taos, New Mexico)

Earthships contain an implicit critique of 'conventional architecture', both a repudiation of aesthetics above functionality and a passionate argument against the concept of building shells that are almost wholly uninhabitable without services being piped in. Their form is dictated by function, though that does not mean that they are ugly – human comfort in every sense is the prime consideration. Mike Reynolds, who has devoted his life to the development of earthships, is so disenchanted with what he views as architecture that he prefers to call himself a 'biotect'. However, he may well agree with Le Corbusier who famously said that "Life is right and the architect is wrong."[1.16] Buildings are meant for human habitation; they are meant for life, and our lives in turn depend on the environment in which we live. Earthships explore the relationship between humans and the natural world, linking life to the elements of nature that sustain our lives. The attractions of earthships seem clear but Mike Reynolds says that the planning establishment, certainly in the USA, has been difficult to win over. "It's hard for the Architects' Board of Examiners when I'm building buildings out of garbage and I'm running sewage through the living room: there are a lot of things they've got problems with." However,

he adds that the culture is changing. "But now", he says, "because of the condition of the planet, they're beating a path to the door."[1.15]

EARTHSHIPS IN THE UK

In the UK sustainability is also becoming well and truly established in the lexicon of UK planners and town hall bosses, along with the pressing need for low or zero carbon emission housing. This has begun to find expression in central government proposals for major sustainability drivers in construction, such as the aforementioned December 2006 announcement of the 'zero carbon new homes' initiative and the voluntary Code for Sustainable Homes. For these proposals to be completely effective, though, they arguably need to be enshrined in law and to move away from a voluntary code to mandatory requirement and enforced legislation across the board. Nonetheless, planning departments are becoming more knowledgeable about sustainable building techniques and technologies, and more supportive of low carbon building projects: the go-ahead for numerous builds across the country, and particularly in London, is evidence of that. Indeed, London has taken a particularly active position through the London Climate Change Agency and the Mayor of London's office.

That there is a pressing need for modern housing in the UK to adopt sustainable strategies is not in doubt. This has been acknowledged by RIBA and the trade association for housing developers, the Home Builders Federation (HBF), whose executive chairman Stewart Baseley made a qualified endorsement of Gordon Brown's announcement in December 2006: "We welcome the challenge made by the Chancellor last week to build all new homes to carbon zero standards within ten years, and we look forward to examining closely the detail of this package of measures. Higher standards will be achieved most effectively through a framework in which government sets clear objectives, industry is given the space to deliver and consumers are on board."[1.17] The need is not only pressing from a global perspective in terms of carbon emissions and their contribution to climate change, but also in terms of specific local shortages of resources (particularly water) in areas of ever-increasing housing density such as south east England. Earthships offer an exemplar of what can be achieved: they are an extreme but entirely appropriate reaction to the increasingly

extreme conditions in which we find ourselves, and in that sense they are completely apposite.

But a note of caution should also be sounded here. While there are a number of promising developments for sustainable housing, the rate of house building in the UK is also set to increase by 23% over the next 20 years, placing a considerable strain on space and resources, and making carbon emission targets extremely difficult to meet.[1.18] Meanwhile organisations such as the HBF is seeking increased deregulation of home building (industry being 'given space to deliver' in Baseley's words) in order to achieve objectives that will surely require significant regulation to be enforced. And a target of zero carbon new homes by 2016 means the hundreds of thousands of homes built between now and then will be built at lower standards than are needed, while the majority of the existing building stock which is being replaced at a negligible rate, remains inefficient and non-sustainable in terms of thermal performance (an average SAP 2001 rating of 52 in 2004), non-renewable electrical demand and other resource use.[1.19] Earthships are no panacea for these times, but they are a significant pointer in the right direction both for new build and retrofitting old stock.

Figure 6: Jacobsen earthship at dusk (Taos, New Mexico)

This book grew out of the building of Earthship Brighton – the first earthship in England – as one of the authors, Mischa Hewitt, was a project manager on the build. Unsurprisingly then, reference is made to Earthship Brighton throughout this book as a primary case study. Reference is also made to the only other earthship in the UK at Kinghorn Loch in Fife. Both of these projects were essentially self-builds, financed through a number of different funds, grants, sponsorship deals and donations, and requiring an enormous amount of personal devotion from the people who actually built them, including large numbers of volunteers. This reflects the grass roots 'bottom-up' nature of earthships and, indeed, much ecological architecture built to date – often designed and constructed by passionate and enthusiastic devotees of the central concepts of sustainability. And the whole sense in which earthships offer a vision of personal empowerment integrates well with what many self-builders would like to derive from their projects. This book, although it is primarily aimed at architects and other building professionals, should also be of interest to self-builders and others with a more general interest in sustainability.

Indeed, one of the fascinating things about earthships, as this introduction has touched upon, is that they provide a melting pot for an enormous array of issues about resources and how we live that are at the heart of contemporary society, including energy, waste, water and food production. That they provide the opportunity for such a wide ranging commentary is certainly part of their appeal. Inevitably, though, it has been tempting to stray into every area upon which the earthship's foundations touch. We have tried to do so in a way that is entirely pertinent to the subject at hand, though there are two observations to make about this. Firstly that this book, in tune with its subject matter, sets out to deliberately explode the myth that buildings exist in some kind of vacuum divorced from their surroundings; building is one of the most obvious and damaging forms of human interaction with our environment and as much as anything the earthship is an exploration of the direct relationship buildings have with this environment. It is therefore necessary to explore as fully as possible all the different components of that relationship from carbon emissions to wastewater. Secondly, the legislative framework that has had an impact on the building of Earthship Brighton is far reaching and can be a significant hurdle to the deployment of new low carbon methods, techniques and technologies, ranging from EU directives about waste, and planning constraints to the 2003 *Energy white paper*.[1.20]

An exploration of this legislation is required to put the earthship in its proper context – in terms of energy, for example, it is impossible to discuss zero carbon building without looking at the government energy strategy and the incentives available for microgeneration. Wherever possible we have tried to place the earthship within the context of UK legislation and building culture and also to relate earthships to other buildings – both those with similar aspirations and housing in the UK in general.

SUMMARY OF CONTENTS

Chapter 2 answers the question of what exactly an earthship is and takes a look at how the concept evolved.

Chapter 3 examines how the earthship uses thermal mass, super insulation and passive solar design principles to fulfil its space heating and cooling requirements. This chapter also incorporates a major study conducted by the University of Brighton into the thermal performance of Earthship Brighton.

Chapter 4 examines how renewable energy is deployed onsite for microgeneration and how effective microgeneration is. This chapter also looks at the implications of offgrid living and a review of government energy strategy.

Chapter 5 is also about offgrid alternatives, although this time with water, both in terms of harvesting rainwater for potable and non-potable uses and recycling water a number of times to gain maximum use from this vastly undervalued resource.

Chapter 6 looks at how the earthship uses waste and low embodied energy materials. It also disentangles the legislation and regulatory position regarding building with waste in the UK.

Chapter 7 uses Earthship Brighton as a case study and takes a detailed look at the construction methods and materials used. This contains key details about site selection, planning and construction that will be particularly essential for potential self-builders.

Box 3

DEFINING A ZERO CARBON HOME

In talking about zero carbon housing it is essential to define exactly what a zero carbon home is – the definition is far from being universally agreed. Here are three different definitions from the government, a developer and an architect.

Government's definition

The government's definition of a zero carbon home taken from the DCLG launch of the zero carbon homes consultation on 13 December 2006, says:

"A zero carbon home is one with 'zero net emissions of carbon dioxide (CO_2) from all energy use in the home'. The definition encompasses all energy use in the home (including energy for cooking, TVs, computers and other appliances) rather than just those energy uses that are currently part of building regulations (space heating, hot water, ventilation and some lighting). It means that over a year there are no net carbon emissions resulting from the operation of the dwelling. This could be achieved either through steps taken at the individual dwelling level or through site wide strategies. So it will not be necessary for each dwelling to have its own microgeneration capacity where development level solutions would be more appropriate." (News release: Towards a zero carbon future).[B1]

Developer's definition

The development company BioRegional's definition of a zero carbon home means to:

1. Reduce the demand for energy through:
   – high levels of insulation and use of natural light and passive heating and ventilation.
   – inclusion of low energy appliances and light fittings in all of the homes.
2. Supply the remaining energy required from renewable sources which do not contribute to the devastating effects of climate change.

BioRegional goes on to say that:

"Whether a development can be zero carbon on its own site or whether it will need to draw renewable energy from the grid will depend on the availability of local resources, for example high wind speeds, sunlight or surplus biomass. All zero carbon developments will need to be connected in to the national grid in order to deal with fluctuations in energy generation and demand. BioRegional's view is that generating all the energy onsite from renewable sources, whilst it is the ideal and attractive option, is not always possible or the best thing to do. It might be better to generate some of the energy offsite or from larger renewable energy plants supplying the wider community. In all cases it is necessary to establish an energy service supplier as developers

themselves are really in a different business. Therefore BioRegional suggests that the government needs to consider how to bring the utility companies into the zero carbon homes consultation.

One other factor which BioRegional believes the government should take into account would be a fairer price for energy produced by small scale renewable energy generators. The renewable energy produced at BedZED or comparable projects – who have to be connected to the grid to even out demand fluctuations – is purchased for a substantially lower price than the energy pulled off the grid. In Germany the price paid is the same whether you are buying or generating and in California a premium is paid for renewable energy. A fairer price would improve the returns on investment for renewable energy producers and encourage a much wider take up." (BioRegional's response to UK government's announcements on zero carbon homes).[B2]

Architect's definition

According to the architectural practice, Zed Factory, the definition of a carbon neutral development is different to this. They say that:

The specification of a 100% carbon neutral development is one in which:

1. All heat and hot water for homes and workplaces is generated from renewable energy sources within site boundaries.
2. The ZED fabric (ie the building fabric) achieves a step change reduction in the need for heat and power, making it possible to harvest a high percentage of passive energy.
3. Enough electricity is generated from renewable sources within the site boundaries to match the annual electrical demand for the entire live/work community.
4. Overall annual CO_2 emissions to atmosphere are zero (biomass is considered to be carbon neutral).[B3]

References and notes

[B1] DCLG (13 December 2006). News release: Towards a zero carbon future. www.communities.gov.uk/index. asp?id=1002882&PressNoticeID=2320.

[B2] BioRegional's response to UK government's announcements on zero carbon homes, 20 December 2006 www.bioregional.com/news%20page/news_stories/ZED/zerocarbon%20201206.htm.

[B3] Dunster B (2006). From A to ZED: Realising zero (fossil) energy developments, (2nd ed). Wallington, Surrey, ZED Factory Ltd.

Chapter 8 is all about the future of earthships, particularly in the UK. Are they going to be a huge phenomenon in themselves or does their significance lie in the lessons that can be learned from them and applied to other forms of design solutions? This chapter also addresses how specific design features need to be modified for the British climate – earthships were founded in a semi-arid part of the USA and tailored specifically for their particular environment. Some of the improvements on the built prototypes in the UK may seek to concentrate on further adaptation to the particular environmental conditions found here.

But whatever the future of earthships is, if we are listening to both what the news and nature appears to be telling us then finding out about these structures is not only of interest, it is absolutely essential as we move into a low carbon building future in a global climate of uncertainty.

REFERENCES AND NOTES

[1.1] Stern N (2006). The economics of climate change: The Stern review. Executive summary (short). www.hm-treasury.gov.uk/media/999/76/CLOSED_SHORT_executive_summary.pdf.

[1.2] www.communities.gov.uk/index.asp?id=1002882&PressNoticeID=2320.

[1.3] EC Directive on the Energy Performance of Buildings (2002/91/EC of 16.12.2002).

[1.4] www.metoffice.gov.uk/corporate/pressoffice/2006/pr20060801.html.

[1.5] www.energywatch.org.uk/help_and_advice/energysmart/index.asp.

[1.6] Architects' Journal (8 July 1999).

[1.7] The BBC reported that the death toll had reached 220 000 on January 20, 2005. http://news.bbc.co.uk/1/hi/world/asia-pacific/4189883.stm.

[1.8] www.newscientist.com/article.ns?id=dn4259.

[1.9] www.nea.org.uk/Policy_&_Research/Fuel_poverty_facts/Excess_winter_mortality. The figures are taken from: Healy, JD, 2003. Excess winter mortality in Europe: a cross country analysis identifying key risk factors. Journal of Epidemiology and Community Health, volume 57, number 10.

[1.10] George Monbiot was talking at the Conway Hall on October 4, 2006 at an event organised by the Campaign Against Climate Change.

[1.11] www.royalsoc.ac.uk/landing.asp?id=1278.

[1.12] DEFRA (2006). UK climate change programme.

[1.13] Architects' Journal (19 June 2003). Earth mover (a profile of Mike Reynolds) by Kevin Telfer, pp18–19.

[1.14] www.metoffice.gov.uk/corporate/library/factsheets/factsheet14.pdf (p11). For New Mexico precipitation, see www.taosproperties.com/info.html. The New Mexico figure is also based on anecdotal reports from Mike Reynolds and other Taos residents.

[1.15] Mike Reynolds' presentation to Green Party councillors at Brighton Town Hall on June 26, 2006.

[1.16] Le Corbusier is originally supposed to have said: 'Vous savez, c'est la vie qui a raison, l'architecte qui a tort'. He is quoted in Philippe Boudon, Lived-in architecture: Pessac Revisited, 1969. Translated by Gerald Onn. The statement is said to have been Le Corbusier's reply upon learning that the housing project he had designed at Pessac had been altered by its inhabitants.

[1.17] Stewart Baseley quoted in a Home Builders Federation press release on December 13, 2006. www.hbf.co.uk (news archive).

[1.18] Office of the Deputy Prime Minister (ODPM) 2006. Statistical release 2006/0042. "The number of households in England is projected to increase from 20.9 million in 2003 to 25.7 million by 2026, an annual growth of 209 000".

[1.19] Department of Communities and Local Government (DCLG) (2006). The energy efficiency of dwellings – initial analysis. p9.

[1.20] DTI (2003). Energy white paper: Our energy future – creating a low carbon economy. London, The Stationery Office.

CHAPTER 2
WHAT IS AN EARTHSHIP?

INTRODUCTION

There have been many unusual speculative answers to the question of 'what is an earthship?' from those who have not previously seen or heard of the buildings. 'Is it some kind of spacecraft?' is one of the more common responses, for example, with headline writers evidently preferring this version of events, judging by the number of times some variant of 'the earthships have landed' have appeared in the press![2.1] It is certainly an unconventional name for a serious building, but it is in many different ways an accurately descriptive epithet for something that might otherwise have been called an 'earth sheltered, sustainable resource strategy, zero carbon dwelling' or some similarly unwieldy phrase. The word earthship is not just about one aspect of construction – 'those buildings made from old car tyres', for example – but describes a holistic and practical approach to sustainable architecture, an introduction to which is given in this chapter. This book goes on to explore all the elements of sustainable construction embodied in earthships in detail. Each one of these elements can be incorporated into a building to make it more sustainable, but taken together they provide a powerful example of a building that deals with many of the pressing ecological issues facing society today.

Figure 7: Hybrid earthship at night (Taos, New Mexico)

LOW CARBON LIVING IN LUXURY

The primary purpose of earthships is as residential structures, designed specifically to provide shelter and homes for people. In antithesis to the majority of mass produced modern housing, though, earthships provide the vital apparatus for human life embedded within the building. By contrast, most modern housing is comprised of thin walled shells that would be completely uninhabitable were it not for centralised grid-derived resources to drive the space heating, electrical input and fresh water that fuel them. And the fundamental – and needless – inefficiency of these homes makes their habitation an expensive business for the occupants who have to pay for all these services to be piped in, with the environment ultimately footing the bill. Perhaps that is an adequate solution if the infrastructure meets certain criteria, but the earthship suggests that there is a better alternative. There is a sense of idealism in the life that the earthship can offer to its occupants; a dream, perhaps, were it not for the fact that many people already live that dream rather than merely fantasise about it.

The dream is this: envisage a building that is, without exaggeration, a passport to freedom, where it is not necessary to work to pay utility bills, because there are none. Your home effortlessly heats itself in winter and cools itself in summer, harvests water every time it rains and recycles that same water for multiple uses. Whenever the sun shines and the wind blows, electrical energy is pumped into your house and stored for your use. The water recycling system allows for the cultivation of numerous edible plants within the building itself, and you are able to live happy in the knowledge that your footprint on the earth produces a negligible level of carbon emissions and uses only bountiful and renewable resources that are flowing freely from nature to sustain your life. The building you live in looks after you and cares for your needs. Ecological living through earthships is not about privation but about an improvement of the quality of life for its inhabitants and their descendants. 'Wake up and smell the coffee!' you might respond. But this is not an impossible dream at all, despite the hurdles faced by the site selection, planning process, construction and capital finance requirements involved in any building. The earthship is an approach to construction combining a number of different elements of sustainability which in fact materially deliver on this dream. It is a totally independent and self-sufficient 'vessel' that heats, cools and powers itself, harvests all its water from the sky and uses plants to treat its sewage. And this is where the descriptive nature of the name earth 'ship' becomes apparent. The earthship has no connection to the water main, the national power grid, the gas main, or sewage system: the utilities that 99.9% of conventional buildings in the UK are tethered to. In essence they are buildings that harness the earth's natural resources to provide all the utilities or building services that are needed to make and sustain a habitable dwelling. Therefore, it could be said that the earthship is 'free floating', somewhat like a yacht or ship that uses only the natural resources of the wind, tide and currents to sail from place to place. Similarly, the earthship uses the sun, wind and rain to achieve its primary aim – to provide comfortable accommodation for its inhabitants. There are certain other implications involved in being an offgrid autonomous home, and these are discussed in the relevant chapters of this book, particularly those on water and renewable energy. But the significant point is that the earthship provides comfort for the occupants from sustainable sources derived directly from the site itself.

SITE HARMONY AND SYNERGY

Using abundant and renewable natural resources harnessed on any site, such as sunlight, wind and rain, immediately draws comparison to 'systems' found in nature. In many ways, the earthship seeks to mimic some of these natural systems that provide excellent lessons in what we might call 'site harmony'. The deciduous tree is a perfect example. It is a solar oriented structure that uses its leaves as solar collectors for harnessing energy. The branches of a tree grow in such a way as to promote the greatest possible exposure of its leaves to the sun so it can collect as much energy as possible. The tree's root system obtains both water and nutrients from the soil and helps in the process of recycling those nutrients as leaves drop off the tree and get absorbed into the soil once more. The wind spreads the seeds of the tree and removes dead branches from its structure. So we can see that the tree is able and in fact, has to, obtain all that

Figure 8: Split level earthship (Taos, New Mexico)

it needs from its immediate site and surroundings. And in using this strategy it has evidently been a highly successful organism that is endemic across the world, despite massive pressures from human intervention. Needless to say, taking only as much as it needs to survive and grow, the tree does not have an observably negative impact on the planet whilst achieving this success, but lives in synergy with its surroundings.

Like trees, the earthship seeks to establish a connection with nature that is not exploitative, but is balanced by using site abundant natural resources to the building's maximum advantage. Whilst the earthship concept is universal, each building needs to be tailored to the site where it is located to take full advantage of the particular characteristics of the unique site environment. For example, the angle of the front glass facade can be tailored to be perpendicular to the angle of the winter sun at its lowest point in the sky to maximise solar gain, and

the roof can be designed to catch either snow melt or rain depending on weather patterns. In temperate climates of the northern hemisphere, all earthships will face south to receive the maximum amount of sunlight available in the colder months, therefore in this respect the main demand onsite choice is that the area must have a south facing aspect. This can be flat or on a south facing slope: the latter characteristic means that the earthship is suitable for developments into steep facing south cliffs.

The most extreme example of how this is possible is the REACH community in Taos, New Mexico which is literally halfway up the side of a steep mountainside. The systems for microgeneration will also be specifically tuned to the particular site with photovoltaic arrays facing south for maximum solar capture, wind turbines being sited in the most advantageous location, with minimal obstacles interfering, and the possibility of employing other forms of site specific generation such as microhydro if there is a stream or river on, or near to, the site (as at Earthship Fife).

As the sun is the generator that fuels our entire planet and its weather systems, it is inevitable that the earthship should try and make best use of its free energy. In fact, as with all sustainable housing in temperate climates, the solar orientation of the earthship is the single greatest factor in ensuring successful passive solar heating. With what is by human standards a virtually inexhaustible power source that provides, according to Godfrey Boyle, more than 10 000 times humanity's current rate of use of fossil and nuclear fuels combined, it seems incredible that more use is not made of the sun in almost all senses.[2.2] The earthship attempts to redress this balance and provides an alternative vision to the current situation where elements – sun, wind and rain – constantly interact with our buildings, yet most of the built stock takes no advantage from that interaction. The earthship, by contrast, gathers and uses all of the resources from immediately around it. The elements that interact with the earthship are either used directly – as passive solar heating, for example – converted into electrical energy, or stored for use as they are needed, including periods when the resource may be scarce, for example storing rainwater to be used during dry periods or heat in the thermal mass during cold.

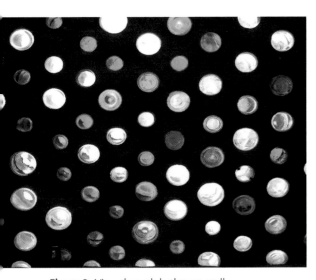

Figure 9: View through bathroom wall (Earthship Brighton)

LIVING WITHIN OUR MEANS

The way in which earthships address the human exploitation of resources, by relating use to the actual physical footprint of the building, provides a solution to the problem of overuse of resources across the developed world, including the UK. As at 2006 the UK uses resources at a rate suggesting that we actually have three planets to plunder rather than just one.[2.3] This is clearly an unsustainable way of living that is also highly carbon-emissions intensive as well as creating other pollutant byproducts and generating massive levels of waste. The earthship, by contrast, seeks to use the resources around it to minimise its environmental impact on the wider world, restricting its resource implications to its own footprint. What you see is what you get. Using only renewable resources that are directly available to a building is one component of what has been called 'one planet living' and is the first goal in any route towards a truly sustainable future.

AUTONOMY AND SELF-SUFFICIENCY

The primacy of site harmony and systems that are able to run independent of networked structures, means that earthships are not just able to be autonomous and self-sufficient but have been specifically designed and powered down to allow human comfort in just such a situation. In fact, this was how they originally evolved in a location where no infrastructure existed, as we shall see in more detail below. But that need for self-sufficiency created a building that by necessity cannot use and does not need more than it has immediately available to it. This sets up a model that is in opposition to the whole concept of large scale infrastructure. Major infrastructure such as the National Grid, mains water and sewage networks, whilst providing stability and security for society, is slow to react to change, expensive to replace or renew and is highly inefficient. It also provides the end user with the impression that it is capable of supplying infinite demand which creates room for very wasteful behaviour. One example of this inefficient infrastructure was seen in the financial year 2005/06 when the water mains controlled by Thames Water leaked on average an astonishing 894 million litres per day, which amounts to the average domestic water consumption for almost 6 million people in the UK.[2.4] That type of inefficiency is emblematic of problems across the board with all types of large scale infrastructure, be it water, electricity or sewage. The earthship, though, does not waste any water; it collects it from rainfall, filters it for potable use and recycles the used water for watering plants and flushing the toilet, before treating the sewage onsite and returning clean water to the environment. And the point with inefficient conveyance of electricity is that the power being lost from the grid is not 'clean power' from renewable sources but, in the main, fossil fuel generated electricity that will in part be derived from power stations that have massive thermal inefficiencies. The net result in many of our power stations is that we are converting the stored chemical energy of precious fossil fuel into plumes of steam and hot air.

That there are various quantitative arguments against centralised infrastructure is without doubt, but it is also the social implications of autonomy and self-sufficiency that are key in the evolution of the earthship concept. Earthships are not just about having a low impact on the environment, but about improving the quality of life for their inhabitants without negative consequences for the environment. This is in itself, of course, an attractive lifestyle proposition for many people. But there is also a significant financial element involved. With highly inefficient homes of the type that constitute almost all of the UK's current building stock, homeowners are paying large, and rapidly increasing, utility bills for space heating, electricity and water. We could think of these houses as being like credit cards with large balances on them that are accumulating debit interest. That 'interest' is the utility bills that need paying every month because the home is too inefficient and badly designed to be able to heat itself and provide the electricity and water needed for its inhabitants. By contrast the earthship could be considered as a savings account with the positive interest being the free natural resources that enable the home to function effectively without any costs beyond the initial capital outlay and a little maintenance.

Perhaps the most significant social aspect of earthships, though, is the sense of personal empowerment that they give to their occupants – in the most literal sense. Homeowners of earthships have taken responsibility for generating their own electricity and regulating their own use of it, for

ensuring that they have enough water and that all the systems in their building are operating satisfactorily. That responsibility should be seen not in a negative, oppressive sense; instead the full tools for life and survival are at the occupant's fingertips, a thrilling alternative, surely, to having an account number to quote down the phone to an indifferent call centre operative when something goes wrong. The earthship, in contrast to the status quo, offers an opportunity to form an unmediated connection with the natural resources that are essential for human life. This bridges the gap that has evolved between people and their environment, a form of alienation that means it is difficult for many people in modern societies to understand their use of natural resources beyond the most clearly manifest reality that water comes out of a tap and gas from a pipe.

THE EVOLUTION OF THE EARTHSHIP IDEA

This unmediated connection with nature was not a choice for the inventor of earthships, Mike Reynolds, who chose to build in a remote area of New Mexico where there was no infrastructure available at all. The buildings he designed had to be self-sufficient or else they would fail completely: a true case of survive or die. It would seem that the necessity to find a solution has certainly been instrumental in achieving a successful design outcome in these terms. But the first impulse for Mike Reynolds' design did not quite derive from the same type of sustainability agenda that is generally accepted as being the principle driver for eco-building today. His first buildings from 1970 were made out of steel cans in a bid to try and recycle some of the massive amounts of waste being generated by society. So he was already experimenting with waste materials as the building blocks for structures. The progression to using recycled tyres as building materials occurred a few years later. Mike Reynolds says that "in the mid-seventies we began looking for ways to build thermal mass into buildings for the purpose of stabilising temperatures. Because we were already building with cans, we found ourselves in the frame of mind to see (about) the possibility of using tyres for buildings".[2.5] This was partially motivated by unfolding energy crises at the time, such as that of the oil shocks in 1973, and

Figure 10: Earthship Fife visitor centre (Kinghorn, Scotland)

concerns about the long term security of fossil fuel supplies, that established the idea of self-sufficiency from the perspective of energy security, as much as from an ecological viewpoint. Security of supply remains a critical issue in the fossil fuel energy industry today and as time goes by becomes more so.

The experiment of building with tyres was a successful one in a number of different ways, from a structural point of view to the fact of embodying thermal mass in buildings, and it started a process of experimentation and evolution that continued for the next 30 years. There are now more than 150 earthships in existence in the USA, mainly around Taos, New Mexico, and numerous other individual earthships spread across the world, including examples in Japan, mainland Europe and the UK. In each new build the idea is to tailor the concept to suit the particular environmental conditions and

Mike Reynolds sees the flexibility and constant evolution of the earthship systems as being part of their intrinsic value, derived from homeowners taking responsibility for their own 'life support'.

The form of an earthship can be very varied, but after all of the different elements are taken into consideration they tend to be fairly similar. The design of Earthship Fife and Earthship Brighton reflect the ecology and lessons learned from the experiences of building and living in Taos. The next generation of earthships in Europe will need to be tweaked in order to maximise their potential for rainwater catchment and solar energy collection. Developing further earthships in temperate climates will help to hone design solutions to fit in with their particular environment as congruently as possible.

AESTHETICS AND FUNCTIONALITY

We have seen, then, that the earthship concept is a universal approach for a building that provides all of the functions that are needed to create a habitable space or shelter. The primacy of function is critical here and little emphasis so far in this book has been placed on how the building actually looks. But it is not true to say that aesthetics are unimportant to earthships, it is just that performance has to come first. It can certainly be argued that this performance in itself has aesthetic value, centred on the principles of harmony, equilibrium and site context that embody design elegance. By contrast, it could be argued that housing which relies on depleting unsustainable resources and as a consequence pollutes the atmosphere and the world around it; housing that is fundamentally divorced from the natural world, is ugly, or at the very least, inharmonious. This debate is at the very heart of what aesthetics mean in architecture, a human activity that is often looked upon as an art form, yet which also has profound implications upon the physical environment that it is clearly so much more. That tension, indeed, is part of the thrill of designing buildings, but it is a tension that in the main has been pulled away from major consideration of those profound implications on the natural world, either through an over emphasis on 'artistic statement' or, more commonly, the 'bank statement' of profit margins.

James Wines in his book *Green Architecture* argues that "nature is an instructive and inspirational influence that can expand the aesthetic horizons of the building arts and confirm the inalienable right of humanity to salvage a place on this planet before it is too late. The mission now in architecture, as in all human endeavour, is to recover those fragile threads of connectedness with nature that have been lost for most of (the 20th) Century. The key to a truly sustainable art of architecture for the new millennium will depend on the creation of bridges that unite conservation technology with an earth centric philosophy and the capacity of designers to transform these integrated forces into a new visual language".[2.6] It is a compelling argument which suggests there needs to be a re-evaluation of the current aesthetic paradigm in architecture and for a significant progression that has more basis and proportion in the human relationship with the natural world with human scale housing. But the earthship also demands that there not just be a 'new visual language' but an emphatic prioritisation of building performance above and beyond the idea of building services being non-sustainable, secondary to form and supplied solely by external agencies. As Mike Reynolds bluntly puts it, "housing should be a result of biology and physics, not a result of design prettiness. I am all for art and design, but if you make a boat really beautiful and it sinks, what the hell use is it?"[2.7]

Generally, the contemporary situation is of function following (and being subservient to form) a form which in terms of numbers of units is actually mainly dictated by cost pressures, rather than the need for artistic statement. The reality, of course, is that housing development is an industrial business where developers need to keep unit costs as low as possible to maintain their profit margins. This would seem to indicate that aesthetics are not important to mass housing anyway – and functionality only up to the level of hitherto inadequate minimum passable building standards – but there are two key points to make about this.

Firstly flagship buildings offer design prototypes and conceptual – and practical – pump priming for industrial scale, mass produced housing. So the blueprint for an aesthetic of zero carbon housing is very much 'up for grabs' with the UK earthships offering one of a limited number of other potential visions for a new performance based visual identity of UK housing. The second point is that there is the same need to redefine profit as there is a need to redefine aesthetics. Just as we might say that a newly designed 'beautiful' building with a massive carbon footprint has a fundamental flaw to it, so we can also say that 'profit' derived from developing unsustainable housing cannot really be profit, for who is it profiting in the long term? True profit is surely to be gained from genuinely sustainable, zero carbon housing that does not damage or deplete the natural resources of the environment in which we all collectively live and will give to our children.

Human comfort in every sense is a key consideration with earthships; they are designed to be self-sustaining shelters for people to live happily in. The aesthetics of the living environment, then, are also immensely important and part of the 'performance' criteria of the building. Two key things that reflect

Figure 11: Staircase in the Estrada earthship (Taos, New Mexico)

and is arguably the key factor in the disassociation of human action with consequences on the natural world eg the link between turning on a light switch in a house and coal being shovelled into a power station furnace 100 miles away. The earthship bridges the gap between humans and the natural environment in which they live and makes clear the direct link between naturally occurring resources and human life – to continue with the same example, in a self-sufficient home when the light switch is turned on the light consumes the finite energy that has been harvested by the householder. This arguably has a beneficial impact on the inhabitants of the building and in aesthetic terms is more of a giant leap, rather than merely a step, forwards.

It has often been said that the earthship is a pioneering building, but in truth it embodies and revives some of the most ancient ideas about human habitation. James Wines explains that "on the most essential levels, troglodyte dwellings and structures made of sun baked mud and other indigenous materials are ecologically friendly. Caves and underground habitats – including the subterranean villages of Shensi and Kansu in China, Cappadocia in Turkey, the Malmata area in Tunisia, and the Siwa region in Egypt – take advantage of virtually all that nature provides. They do not impose unreasonably on their environment, they do not negatively affect regional ecology, and they do not require high levels of energy consumption for heating or cooling since (they have) a consistently comfortable interior temperature".[2.6] The earthship in this sense is an echo from the past, a return to the pre-fossil fuel age, although its application finds expression in post industrial technologies and materials that allow the most pragmatic realisation of performance related sustainable goals in the 21st Century. Mike Reynolds argues that "a sustainable home must make use of indigenous materials, those occurring naturally in the local area. For thousands and thousands of years, housing was built from found materials such as rock, earth, reeds and logs. Today, there are mountains of byproducts of our civilization that are already made and delivered to all areas. These are the natural resources of the modern humanity".[2.5] Hence the reason that earthships are built from tyres, bottles and other low embodied energy salvaged materials rather than the hitherto more usual idea of ecological building materials such as timber, stone and straw bales.

this and that make enormous qualitative impacts to the aesthetics of habitation are the vast amount of sunlight that floods into earthships through the massive south facing windows, and the fact that plants are an integrated part of the internal structure of the building. These are strong aesthetic and ergonomic statements within the earthship that enhance the experience of the building's inhabitants. Enhancement of the living experience could also be viewed through the eyes of eco-psychology – a branch of psychology that suggests that people have become increasingly alienated from the natural environment, the condition of which governs the viability of human survival. According to eco-psychology, this alienation is an underlying cause of many psychological problems in developed societies

Box 4

MIKE REYNOLDS: BIOGRAPHICAL SKETCH

The charisma of earthships as structures surely has a great deal to do with their creator, the 'missionary, maverick, revolutionary, bad boy of architecture', Michael E Reynolds.[B1] Mike Reynolds has been evolving designs for earthships for more than 30 years in New Mexico and has the driven vision of a true pioneer. That vision has had a long history of flying in the face of convention, not helped, he remarks, by the fact that he is "building buildings out of garbage (and) running sewage through the living room".[B2] This is the kind of straight talking style that is characteristic of Mike Reynolds and has earned him numerous friends as well as the inevitable opposition you might also expect. Indeed, he is a veteran of run-ins with the authorities.

He graduated in architecture from the University of Cincinnati in 1969 and at that time was already thinking about how architecture could better respond to the environmental challenges facing it. The main driver at the outset was a form of disgust at the amount of waste that was being created by society; 'waste' that could instead be reused to good effect – to make buildings with, for example. So he started creating structures out of rubbish – mainly bottles and steel cans – before later experimentations with rubber tyres. The thermal mass concept became obviously pertinent as the fuel crises of the early 1970s hit the USA and the long term security of supply of fossil fuels began to be regarded as a serious issue. So the home that did not require heating from fossil fuel sources became more of a sought after goal and the evolution of the earthship began and kept going until it became the fully integrated – but still evolving – building concept it is today.

Mike Reynolds sees the earthship as an essentially organic unit; a "water producing, heat producing, food producing organism that coexists with and sustains the human organism" and one that can also evolve new systems on an individual dwelling basis.[B2] He therefore feels that the design has resilience in terms of being capable of adaptation to suit particular circumstances.

Clearly he is not a 'typical architect', if such a thing exists, but Mike Reynolds is also not even what you could call a desk based architect. He claims to love few things more than pounding tyres – a highly labour intensive process of packing earth densely into the tyres that will form the basic structure of earthships – and he is out onsite far more than he is sat behind a desk. He is as much – if not more – of a practitioner as he is an architect and in fact he has shunned the title of his profession, preferring instead to call himself a biotect. However, it could be claimed that it is the other way around and that the title of architect has, in fact, shunned Mike Reynolds as he was forced to give up his licence in New Mexico in 2000 due to a series of run-ins with the New Mexico Board of Examiners for Architects.

But Mike Reynolds seems to have more important things on his mind. "While other people and professionals may take this further in different ways" he says, "we're right now planting the seeds, and, if humanity is to survive, they will have to do something like this." He is obsessive and indefatigable, a livewire of concentrated energy capable of inspiring audiences at talks and volunteers on building sites who came to see what all the fuss was about. "Mike Reynolds is a kind of outlaw, and he's angry." wrote Henry Shukman in the Observer.[B1] Why is he so angry? Mainly because he feels too little is being done to promote zero carbon, self-sufficient buildings, and to remedy man's brutality to his environment. "The certain uncertainty staring at us in the future should be enough to cause all political figures to take what would be considered extreme steps to protect the people from water, food and energy shortages," he says. "This would involve opening doors in building regulations to allow buildings to emerge that take care of people regardless of whether conventional public utilities are available or not. Earthships can make it so more people can simply survive in an uncertain future, but if introduced in a large way soon enough, they can change that future."[B3]

References and notes

[B1] Shukman H (19 March 2006). New age New Mexico. The Observer.

[B2] Telfer K (19 June 2003). Earth mover (a profile of Mike Reynolds). Architects' Journal, pp18-19.

[B3] Email from Mike Reynolds to Kevin Telfer, January, 2007.

Figure 12: Adobe arches in the Kurnizi earthship (Taos, New Mexico)

MODULAR DESIGN – DIFFERENT TYPES OF EARTHSHIP

In terms of specific designs of earthships there is the potential to create numerous different forms using the central principles embodied by the building; the approach is not prescriptive but pragmatic. However, there have been a limited number of variations built to date. These are the rectilinear 'packaged nest' earthship, which in the USA include options for prefabrication, and modular earthships based on a combination of 'U-shapes' and (circular) 'huts' . The U-module means that there is mass on three sides and multiple modules combined can create an entire dwelling. Earthship Brighton, by contrast, is composed of a 'nest', that constitutes the major part of the building, and a circular hut that is the office space.

ELEMENTS OF SUSTAINABLE CONSTRUCTION

Perhaps the major underlying principle of sustainable building as established at the Rio Earth Summit of 1992 is to create building solutions that provide a high standard of living today without compromising the opportunity of others to have a high standard of living tomorrow.[2.8] The five core elements of sustainable construction that embody this principle are all present in earthships and provide the main chapter headings of this book. Each chapter explores a different element in depth and explores the various aspects of the interaction between the earthship and its immediate environment, and how the earthship takes full advantage of its situation.

The main elements of sustainable building in earthships are: use of low impact materials in construction, passive solar design for space heating, energy efficiency and renewable energy sources for day-to-day electrical and hot water demand, and water conservation measures including rainwater harvesting for water supply and onsite wastewater treatment and recycling, using plants to filter out impurities. All of these features concern themselves with the reduction of the level of inputs required through demand management which then allows the remaining demand to be more easily met by renewable resources which are readily available from the site.

These elements combined as a whole create a holistic building approach with a low environmental impact and outstanding 'green credentials'. These characteristics that are inherent in an earthship are not unique and can be found in other building styles and types. Other design concepts that share similar values to the earthship approach are:

- The ZED standard
- WWF and BioRegional's concept of one planet living
- The Passivhaus system
- Association for Environment Conscious Building's (AECB) 'Silver', 'Gold' and 'Platinum' standards
- The work of Robert and Brenda Vale including the Hockerton Housing Project.[2.9]

These standards embody an implicit acknowledgement that buildings are a legacy left for future generations and should be a gift rather than a curse. The more efficient the form of the building fabric is, the better the legacy that is left and visa versa. In the UK, as in most parts of the developed world, the legacy is a relatively static stock of buildings bequeathed by our ancestors, which have a low turnover rate of replacement. In England the total figure of this existing stock is about 21.8 million homes and in the UK overall this figure grows to around 25 million. And the government says that around 70% of the housing stock that will be standing in 2050 has already been built.[2.10] In a sense, then, the 'sexy' part of tackling climate change through buildings is in new build, whereas the real challenge lies in addressing the fundamental inefficiencies inherent in the built stock already in existence ie retrofitting. Microgeneration, improved insulation, energy saving measures and small scale renewable thermal and electrical energy networks may all prove to have a role in improving the existing stock, incentivised by government fiscal measures.

But the principal concern of architects and developers is in the area of new build. And while many of the principles in demand reduction and microgenerative strategies from the earthship may be identified as suitable for retrofitting, the building's development of sustainable strategies over the last 30 years should have a keen influence on those architects' and developers' production of new build zero carbon designs and practices.

An announcement from the Treasury and DCLG in December 2006 saw the launch of the Code for Sustainable Homes that purportedly aims to bring standards for new build to zero carbon levels by 2016. This is set against the backdrop of a large demand for new build in the UK with the rate of household formation set to increase by 23% by 2025.[2.11] Architects and developers face major challenges to achieve the new building standards, particularly due to the endemic non-sustainable culture of building practice that has hitherto existed in the UK. However, the earthship has a role to play in demonstrating the employment of the following key tenets of sustainable building that should also be embodied in the mass housing of the future. The following headings briefly outline the elements from the perspective of an earthship. More detail is added in the chapters that follow.

USE OF LOW IMPACT MATERIALS IN CONSTRUCTION

In the complete life cycle analysis of a building the embodied energy in the materials in construction are generally less than 3% of the total energy used. However, once the building becomes low to zero carbon the figure increases and becomes far more significant. Reducing the embodied energy of the materials used in the construction of the earthship is one of the primary aims and the concept uses a variety of 'waste' materials from reclaimed timber and masonry to recycled glass bottles, tin cans and used car tyres. The UK throws away over 48 million car and van tyres a year and the Landfill Directive that came into full force in July 2006 has completely banned them from landfill.[2.12] When referring to used car tyres Mike Reynolds comments "We have been unknowingly mass producing and stockpiling the ideal building materials for the future. The

Figure 13: Hut wall construction (Earthship Brighton)

time has come to begin using them."[2.5] A 130 m² earthship would typically use 1000 or 10 tonnes of used car tyres for the construction of its walls. First hand materials such as structural grade Forest Stewardship Council (FSC) timber are used as well and in these incidences a number of criteria are used to source or specify the material, such as the performance, manufacturing process, energy embodiment and proximity to site.

Passive solar design

Removing the need for external inputs during the design phase rather than looking for a solution after the problem has been invented is a principle of good design which is promoted in the earthship. These external inputs can be removed by the deployment of a number of considerations for the building fabric or envelope such as passive solar design, super insulation and use of appropriate

dense materials to give the building a suitable level of thermal mass; this takes full advantage of any solar gain by storing any heat that is harvested. With the design of conventional buildings within current building regulations, sustainability measures are often introduced to the scheme after the fundamental design has been shaped, meaning that environmental concerns become secondary or what can be called 'added' value rather than 'core value'. The key with the earthship approach is to remove demand, before trying to realise that demand through renewable or sustainable methods. Renewable energy, whether on or offsite, harnessed to meet a demand that could have been designed out at the concept stage of a construction project is a waste of energy that could be put to better use elsewhere.

Earthships are highly efficient principally because they remove the conventional need for vast amounts of space heating. The earthship reduces its demand for external energy inputs because the structure itself is designed to harvest heat which is the type of energy that most of the gas and electricity supplied to conventional buildings is converted to. The rammed tyre walls of the earthship are earth sheltered with over 1 m thickness of rammed earth used as a backfill behind the tyre wall. Behind the earth shelter is a 'thermal wrap' of rigid insulation that embraces the building and makes the thermal mass of rammed tyres and earth act as a storage heater. Just like a stone wall on a hot day the rammed tyre walls retain heat and release it again when the building cools. The thick walls coupled with lots of insulation stabilise the earthship to maintain a comfortable temperature in any season by remaining hot in winter and cool in summer.

Renewable power

The biggest energy demand in residential buildings is heat for space heating, and as the earthship deals with this through thermal mass coupled with super-insulation it is relatively easy to generate the electricity needed for other activities from renewable sources. The earthship has no connection to the National Grid and no fossil fuel is consumed for electricity generation or water heating. Instead electricity is generated onsite with renewables and stored in a battery bank before distribution in the building. This contrasts sharply with conventional buildings, in which centralised systems are vital for all functions and to make the building fit for habitation. Earthship Brighton uses four renewable technologies for these ends; photovoltaic panels, a wind turbine, solar thermal panels and a wood pellet stove as a back up boiler. Earthship Fife uses a couple of these technologies and has a microhydro turbine as well.

Rainwater harvesting

The earthship has no connection to the water mains, but instead relies on rainfall, demand management and water conservation to make the water harvested go as far as possible. The roof collects water and channels it through a pre-filter before storing it in underground tanks. The storage capacity tends to be larger than most domestic rainwater harvesting systems, as there is no mains back up for dry periods. The rainwater harvesting system coupled with an economical usage regime and greywater recycling is more than enough for the needs of residents.

Figure 14: Blackwater treatment (Earthship Fife)

The earthship approached is based on using the appropriate tool for the job. The water is purified in a two stage filtration process to reflect the fact that over 90% of water consumed in residential building is used for non-potable activities. With the relatively high levels of rainfall in the UK, most buildings are very well placed to collect and use rainwater onsite and thus have a lower reliance on a centralised water main.

Using plants to treat waste

In an earthship, grey and blackwater are dealt with separately and all wastewater is treated onsite. The wastewater or greywater that is generated by the sinks and shower is treated with indoor planters or 'living machines', located next to the south facing windows. The plants thrive in conditions of sunlight and nutrient rich water and clean the water through natural processes such as transpiration, evaporation and oxygenation by their roots. All plants work well in the planters, but some 'hardier' species with deeper root systems are good to start with; including bananas, avocados and geraniums. After

being cleaned, the 'recycled' water is then stored in a sump, which is then fed to the toilet cistern for flushing. All blackwater leaves the earthship to settle in a septic tank before overflowing to a reedbed or other system for treatment.

Mike Reynolds is currently exploring a sixth criterion for earthships through the possibility of growing food all year round through the greywater systems. The main example of this building is the Phoenix, built in New Mexico, which has a double greenhouse at the front to allow a far larger area for food production, but also acts as additional thermal buffer. In colder climates the thermal performance of the earthship can be improved by the addition of a greenhouse which acts a buffer, but also as an 'airlock' to reduce thermal loss when the occupants leave or enter the building.

CONCLUSION

In summary the earthship is a building that combines a number of different strands of sustainable building practice in an integrated, holistic approach. It provides a powerful critique of much of present residential building design that is predominantly inefficient, vulnerable to the elements and dependent on centralised infrastructure. The earthship, by contrast, is a self-sufficient offgrid structure that has all its functions embedded within its architecture and interacts effectively with renewable natural resources to provide a comfortable zero carbon home for its inhabitants. It also bridges the gap between people and the natural environment, which offers both psychological benefits for the inhabitants and heightened awareness of human impacts upon our surroundings.

REFERENCES AND NOTES

[2.1] See, for instance, the strapline of the article about Mike Reynolds in the Architects' Journal, 19 June 2003, p 18: The earthships have landed – not aliens from another planet, but self-contained, environmentally friendly dwellings that their creator says points to the future.

[2.2] Boyle G (ed.) (2004). Renewable energy. Oxford, Oxford University Press.

Figure 15: Greywater planter (Earthship Fife)

[2.3] Desai P, King P (2006). One planet living: a guide to enjoying life on our one planet. Bristol, Alastair Sawday Publishing Co. Ltd.

[2.4] As reported by the BBC, see http://news.bbc.co.uk/1/hi/business/5101434.stm.

[2.5] Reynolds M (1990). Earthship volume 2: Systems and components. Taos, New Mexico, Solar Survival Press.

[2.6] Wines J (2000). Green architecture: The art of architecture in the age of ecology. London, Taschen.

[2.7] Telfer K (19 June 2003). Architects' Journal. Earth mover (a profile of Mike Reynolds), pp18-19.

[2.8] Report of the United Nations conference on environment and development (Rio de Janeiro, 3 to 14 June 1992). Principle 3 states "The right to development must be fulfilled so as to equitably meet developmental and environmental needs of present and future generations." See www.un.org/documents/ga/conf151/aconf15126-1annex1.htm).

[2.9] For ZED standard see: Dunster, B 2006. From A to ZED: Realising zero (fossil) energy developments. Second edition. Wallington, Surrey; ZED Factory Ltd. For Passivhaus see www.passivhaus.org.uk/index.jsp?id=668. For the work of Brenda and Robert Vale see The new autonomous house, Thames and Hudson, 2000. For One planet living see reference [2.3] For AECB see www.aecb.net.

[2.10] DCLG (2006). The energy efficiency of homes – initial analysis p 1.

[2.11] DCLG statistical release 2006/0042: "The number of households in England is projected to increase from 20.9 million in 2003 to 25.7 million by 2026, an annual growth of 209,000".

[2.12] For used tyre statistics see: www.wrap.org.uk/construction/tyres/dti_used_tyre_statistics/index.html.

Earthship Brighton under construction, glazing recently installed and footing built from recycled glass bottles

CHAPTER 3
THERMAL MASS

INTRODUCTION

Annually buildings are responsible for approximately 50% of the UK's total carbon footprint of 684 million tonnes of carbon dioxide (mt CO_2). Within this figure residential buildings account for 27% or 175 mt CO_2: this means not only that almost a third of the UK's carbon footprint comes directly from people's homes, but this sector is the third single biggest polluter after transport and power generation: there is clearly a lot of work to do here.[3.1] Delving into the detail of the 27% residential figure, space heating is responsible for around 57% of domestic consumption, with another 25% for water heating, giving a combined total of 82% or 144 mt CO_2 per year of the UK's total carbon footprint. The rest is accounted for by lighting, gadgets and general electrical demand. The proportion of these figures varies in commercial and public buildings. However, overall this means that people heating their homes in winter and heating water all year accounts for over a fifth of the total UK carbon footprint.

Although these figures are arresting, a certain amount can be attributed to people's behaviour. It is certainly possible that a thermostat set a degree or so lower or a jumper worn here or there may save on CO_2 emissions but this cannot be the whole story: there must be another way to reduce the level of energy needed to heat people's homes. This chapter identifies and reviews a number of strategies for reducing the need for space heating and cooling in domestic buildings that have been deployed in various buildings around the UK and Europe, and how they relate to and are used in earthships.

Water heating is discussed in chapter 4. After a brief review of the strategies of passive solar design, thermal mass and super insulation the rest of this chapter is devoted to the University of Brighton's report: The Brighton Earthship: Evaluating the thermal performance (in partnership with Durabuild) written by Professor Andrew Miller, University of Brighton. This aspect of the Earthship Brighton project is crucial to understanding how the building is really working and how the performance can be improved, and it also highlights a wider issue for the deployment of zero carbon housing over the next decade. In the immediate context it lays the performance of the earthship open to independent scrutiny and these objective results are where lessons can be learned. Without a consistent inexpensive independent monitoring scheme in place for all buildings, we will be in grave danger of falling into the gap between design on the drawing board and what actually gets built, or believing the potentially wild claims of the inevitable zero carbon snake oil salesman and the underperforming technologies and buildings they may leave in their wake.

None of the strategies discussed in this chapter are new, and the deployment of them in earthships is not unique: there are plenty of other examples of buildings in the UK, a few notables including the Hockerton Housing Project and the now infamous BedZED, that demonstrate that they are all viable, easily designed and incorporated into new builds. However, this still leaves the 25 million homes in the UK emitting 27% of the UK's CO_2. While we must focus on these techniques to deliver a far higher standard in the millions of homes that will be built over the next 20 years, the real challenge lies in the old building stock and these techniques are not easily retrofitted.

PASSIVE SOLAR DESIGN IN EARTHSHIPS

The sun is so powerful that its energy drives all of the weather systems and ocean currents on earth. Do we need to invent a more powerful energy source than that? Outside of the earth's atmosphere the amount of energy radiating from the sun is the equivalent of 1.2 kW/m². By the time the light has been diffused though the ozone layer and atmosphere, it is reduced down to around 0.8 kW/m² on a clear summer's day. On average, when it is evened out over the rest of the year with clouds taken into consideration, the sun's energy is a mere 0.35 kWm². Our buildings are bathed in this light; the key question is how to ensure that they take maximum advantage from this encounter. There are a number of factors that influence the amount of energy a building can harvest from the sun. These are orientation, obstacles and shading and amount of glazing. While solar energy can be collected from almost any direction the solar gain is by far the strongest from the south (in the northern hemisphere), and weaker from the east and west. From the north the thermal loss far outweighs the thermal gain although this phenomenon in itself can be ideal for other types of building, for example work units. In the temperate northern climate this means that the earthship must be orientated to the south to maximise the opportunity for solar gain, although the building can be slightly facing the east to capture the morning sun. All glazing is from floor to ceiling and there is no glazing on the north and west sides (Table 1).

The lack of glazing on the north face minimises the thermal loss from this area but means that the further away from the front south facing glazing the darker it gets. Generally the depth of the earthship module is calculated by the penetration of the sun during winter; ideally the sun at the winter solstice should hit the base of the back wall. The design of interior layout needs to reflect this to carefully avoid creating dark areas which require extra lighting during the day. The layout of an earthship places rooms next to the amenities that use them, for example the kitchen next to the greywater planter at the front so that the greywater from the sink has to travel a minimum distance and there is lots of natural light during the day. Unfortunately Earthship Brighton has not managed this and even with the addition of a sunpipe the kitchen area is dim during the day. The design of the earthship has openable skylights at the highest point of the roof, as part of the ventilation system, which tend towards the back of the structure; however, the daylight they provide may need supplementing with sunpipes to increase the natural light level. With so much solar gain there is an opportunity for the earthship to overheat and become uncomfortable, but the thermal mass (described under the heading 'Thermal mass and thermal wrap in earthships') stabilises temperatures and, coupled with the natural convection ventilation system, ensures that overheating does not occur. The ventilation system is outlined in detail in chapter 7.

The real advantage in passive solar design is that the building structure or fabric is designed to harness and retain heat. As described in the outline above,

Figure 16: Thermal wrap installation (Earthship Brighton)

Table 1: Glazing to floor area ratio in Earthship Brighton and Earthship Fife

Earthship	Facade	Gross floor area (m²)	Area of glazing (m²)	Ratio (%)
Brighton	South	135.00	36.00	27.0
	East	135.00	4.00	3.0
Fife	South	31.50	9.00	28.5

heat – space and water heating – comprises 82% of the energy demand of a building. If the sun's energy can be used directly for this then there is no conversion loss from other energy sources and therefore efficiency is very high compared to heating using electricity or gas. Earthship Brighton uses two ways of collecting solar energy: in a large expanse of south facing glass and a trombe wall in the hut module. The trombe wall works by the sun heating the air and tyre wall directly behind the glass. The hot air then rises by convection through the holes at the top to heat the space, and cooler air is drawn through the holes at the base of the wall. The holes can be plugged for control at night, overcast days or during summer. In both methods of harvesting heat, direct solar gain and a trombe wall, the warmth is stored in thick thermal mass walls.

Figure 17: Solar gain section (Earthship Brighton)

THERMAL MASS AND THERMAL WRAP IN EARTHSHIPS

The earthship is a very heavyweight construction. The whole building can be cut into a south facing slope, as Earthship Brighton and Earthship Fife have been, or sheltered with earth on a flat piece of land. In either instance the walls, rammed tyres and rammed earth are about 2 m thick and offer a very large thermal store or 'battery' for winter. The tyre wall mass is a loadbearing structure as well, serving a dual purpose. Behind the backfill berm is a 100 mm 'thermal wrap' of rigid insulation which surrounds the building and isolates the thermal mass of rammed tyres and earth, making it act as a storage heater. Just like a stone wall on a hot day the rammed tyre walls retain heat and release it again when the building cools. This principle follows the law of thermodynamics and the earthship is merely exploiting it on a building size scale, capturing heat and storing it; the heat then balances out to find thermal equilibrium. The thick walls coupled with lots of insulation enable the earthship to maintain a comfortable temperature in any season – the building's temperature is stabilised to remain hot in winter and cool in summer. However, although effective, the thickness of the walls has serious implications for the amount of land required per earthship (Figure 16).

Figure 18: Limiting solar gain in summer (Earthship Brighton)

Figure 19: Release of heat from thermal mass (Earthship Brighton)

Figure 20: Convection through Earthship Brighton

Increasingly, a stable indoor temperature makes a property far more comfortable in summer. Given that 9 of the 10 hottest years on record occurred between 1997 and 2006, the need for this stability and the avoidance of energy hungry air conditioning will surely become even more important. Mass of this size, with its large repository of heat provides temperature stability through diurnal fluctuations, but is a lot slower to react than thinner mass. Table 2 summarises the amount of thermal mass in the walls of Earthship Brighton and Earthship Fife (Figures 17 to 20 – section diagrams of Earthship Brighton).

Neither of the earthships that have been built so far has underfloor insulation and that is why the floor slab was not included in calculation in Table 2: only the mass of the walls have been included here. It was a deliberate design decision in both instances to tap into the earth's core ground temperature. Earthships are dug into the ground, below the frost line, to access the natural temperature of the earth. This varies from place to place but the principle is that it is much easier to raise the basic temperature from 10 to 12°C to a comfortable temperature than for a similar structure built above ground. Once again this consideration creates limitations on the type of land that can be developed: to build an 'earthship estate' a south facing hill would be required; if built on a flat piece of ground the estate would need a very large gross area per unit, well

below the minimum guidance set in planning policy of 30 units per hectare.

Another factor with the lack of underfloor insulation is that there is an opportunity for large amounts of thermal loss through the floor. If the stable temperature of the earth is lower than the temperature of the thermal mass in the walls or air temperature then the floor becomes a thermal sink, although this factor will vary considerably depending on the soil and moisture content that the earthship is built into. Once the sun's heat is inside the earthship and has been stored in the mass, its movement needs to be carefully controlled and heat loss restricted when heating is the priority.

SUPER INSULATION IN EARTHSHIPS

The classic definition of a super insulated building is one that is so well insulated that the heat gains from the sun, the occupants, lighting, electrical appliances and cooking are enough to supply all the heat required. Needless to say this is far above and beyond Part L of the Building Regulations. The earthship aims to do this; however, as previously mentioned, there is no insulation under the floor slab. Table 3 summarises the U-values of the various elements of Earthship Brighton. Table 4 summarises the glazing used in Earthship Brighton.

A common addition to the standard earthship design is a greenhouse or conservatory. This acts as a thermal buffer for the nest. The angle of the glass is perpendicular to the sun during winter and provides solar shading in summer by reducing solar gain and glare. Thermal gain must outweigh thermal loss (Figure 22). The design of the greenhouse at Earthship Brighton does not cover the entire front face leaving an area of the nest module that has only one double glazed unit. The design could be modified so that the greenhouse stretches all the way along to extend the thermal buffer which would enhance the performance and reduce the heat loss from the nest at night. Another addition could be insulated shutters on the inside vertical face of glass. This brief discussion of passive solar design, thermal mass and super insulation outlines the form of the earthship. The study that follows demonstrates the actual temperature readings that have been taken over an 18-month period.

Figure 21: Installation of Rockwell Hardrock insulation (Earthship Brighton)

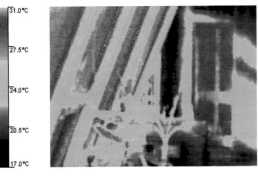

Figure 22 (above and left): Thermographic images of Earthship Brighton taken during the day

Table 2: Volume and mass in walls of Earthship Brighton and Earthship Fife

Earthship	Module	Floor area (m²)	Mass area (m²)	Internal volume (m³)	Mass* (m³)
Brighton	Nest	80.0	54.0	200.0	135.0
	Hut	12.5	23.0	31.3	58.0
Fife	U	31.5	40.5	78.8	101.3

* The assumption is that the thermal mass is 2 m in depth and the tyre is 700 mm and 1300 mm packed out with rammed earth/chalk.

Table 3: Summary of fabric U-values in Earthship Brighton

Element	U-value (W/m²K)	Achieved by
Roof: hut	0.14	200 mm Rockwool Roll and Xtratherm Thin-R pitched roof board
Roof: nest	0.07	30 mm Hard Rock dual density board and 600 mm Rockwool Roll
Thermal wrap (walls)	0.029	100 mm X2i Yelofoam
Windows: interior	2.0	Saint Gobain Solaglas
Windows: exterior	1.1	Saint Gobain Solaglas

Table 4: Specification of glass in Earthship Brighton

	Double glazed unit component			Light transmittance	U-value (W/m²K)
	Inner pane	Gap	Outer pane		
Internal	4 mm	16 mm	4 mm Planitherm Futur N*	62%	2.0
External	7.5 mm laminated	16 mm Argon with Swiss spacer	6 mm Planitherm Futur N*	56%	1.1

* Low e-coating.

THE BRIGHTON EARTHSHIP: EVALUATING THE THERMAL PERFORMANCE

By Professor Andrew Miller, Centre for Sustainability of the Built Environment, University of Brighton

The opportunity for monitoring Earthship Brighton presented itself in April 2003. This was an opportunity for long term monitoring of natural thermal storage in a building designed to take advantage of seasonal storage of heat gains. The building was therefore fitted with a total of 24 temperature sensors buried in the thermal store and in the floor, three internal and one external air temperature sensors, two humidity sensors and a solorimeter measuring incident solar radiation (Figure 23).

During the whole study there were minor problems with monitoring due to undetected errors in the data logging system and at one stage vandalism of the external equipment. However, the data collected, some of which are presented here, provide us with a better understanding of the operation of a building utilising the earthship design principle of 'glass and mass'.

Temperature sensors in the tyre wall

The construction of the thermal storage to the rear of the building consists of the tyre wall plus a further thickness of approximately 1300 mm of rammed chalk before a layer of insulation and waterproof membrane which separates the structure from the surrounding earth.

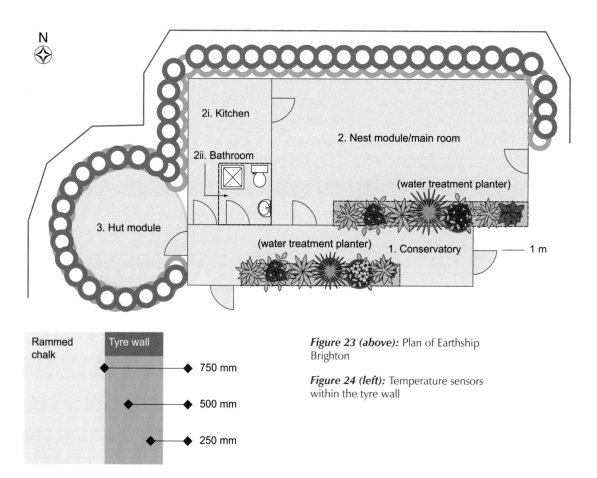

Figure 23 (above): Plan of Earthship Brighton

Figure 24 (left): Temperature sensors within the tyre wall

Temperature sensors were installed in nine positions in the tyre wall to the rear of the main living space. They were positioned at heights of 0.63 m, 1.26 m and 1.89 m above floor level inside the building and at depths of 250 mm, 500 mm and 750 mm into the thermal store as illustrated in Figure 24.

A further nine sensors were installed in similar locations within the tyre wall to the side of the kitchen. This was an attempt to identify the uniformity of conditions throughout the thermal store as within the kitchen the wall is unlikely to be warmed from direct incidence of solar radiation. These measurements represent the first long term monitoring of the thermal store within earthship design.

Anecdotal evidence points to the conclusion that the thermal battery effect of the tyre wall takes two years to reach stability and maximum effectiveness. One of the objectives of the University of Brighton research has been to gather empirical data to investigate this.

Monitored results

Earthship Brighton has been constructed as a visitor centre and as such experiences different internal gains from those of an occupied house. It will also have different requirements for thermal comfort and ventilation compared to a family dwelling. Monitoring at this stage, however, was simply to identify the natural thermal performance of the building.

The building envelope was complete and the monitoring instrumentation was installed in autumn 2004. However, the building, which was reliant on volunteer labour for construction, at that time had not been finished and occupied as a visitor centre. All the results should therefore be considered to be affected by these conditions although they are a very good indication of the passive response of the building.

Initial results from December 2004 demonstrate the thermal performance of the earthship and the relative stability of the inside temperature where no traditional space heating is provided. Under external conditions that varied between -3°C and 12°C, temperatures within the conservatory never fell below 9°C whereas they reached a peak of over 22°C. Within the main room (the nest) temperatures were more stable ranging between 11°C and 18°C over the same time period.

Clearly the internal temperatures had not reached suitable conditions for thermal comfort within

a dwelling, but there were no occupants in this building and no internal gains. Internal air temperatures in both the conservatory and the main room, together with the external air temperature at the time are plotted in Figure 25.

Solar radiation transmitted through the glass serves to heat the surfaces surrounding the room and indirectly to warm the air within the space. The relationship between the incident solar radiation and the internal air temperatures are seen in Figure 26. These measurements were taken during the first winter of monitoring, January 2005.

The internal air temperatures rise rapidly in response to the solar radiation transmitted through the glass. However, during winter, when the altitude of the sun is low, much of the radiation will be incident on the thermal store forming the back wall of the main room. A high proportion of this solar radiation is absorbed by the surface and serves to maintain the long term temperature of the thermal store.

At the time of writing, data are available for the first 18 months after the installation of sensors (November 2004 to April 2006). The break of continuity of the graphs presented in Figures 27 (and Figure 30) is due to a logging error, for a period of approximately four weeks during the early summer and again over the New Year period 2006, when monitoring lapsed. The trends, however, are clear and provide evidence of the seasonal warming of the thermal store.

Average temperatures in the tyre wall

In Figure 27 the average of all nine sensors in the tyre wall is presented, indicating the overall performance of the thermal store. During the period between November 2004 and early spring 2006 the thermal store temperature dropped by over 5°C and rises to a peak of over 9°C above this by late summer. At the end of the first 12 months monitoring the thermal store temperature remained 2°C higher than at the beginning.

The results show that the average temperature of the thermal store falls steadily from November to March, effectively supplying the heat that is maintaining stable conditions within the occupied space. From March through to September, however, there is a net gain of energy stored within the wall.

During 2005, the second year of monitoring the minimum temperature of the thermal store was

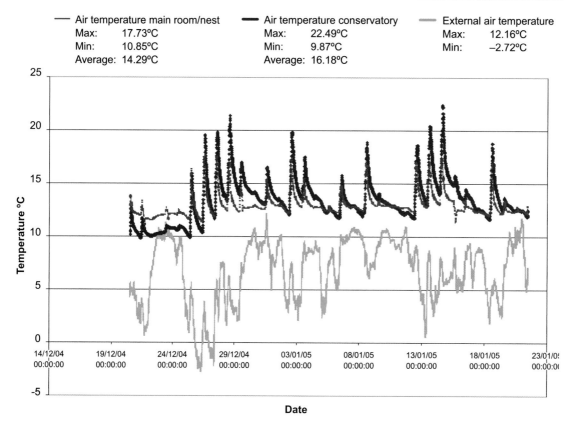

Figure 25: Recorded external and internal temperatures

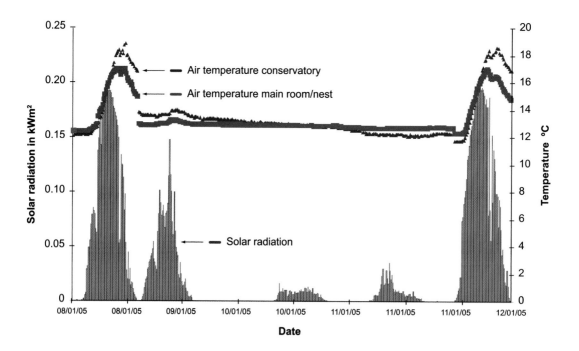

Figure 26: Relationship between incident solar radiation and internal air temperatures

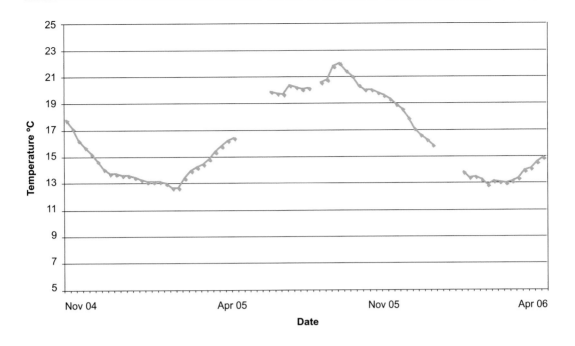

Figure 27: Average thermal store temperatures in the nest module/main room

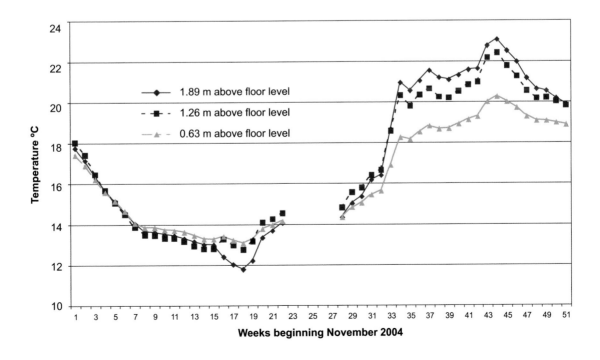

Figure 28: Vertical temperature gradient within the thermal store

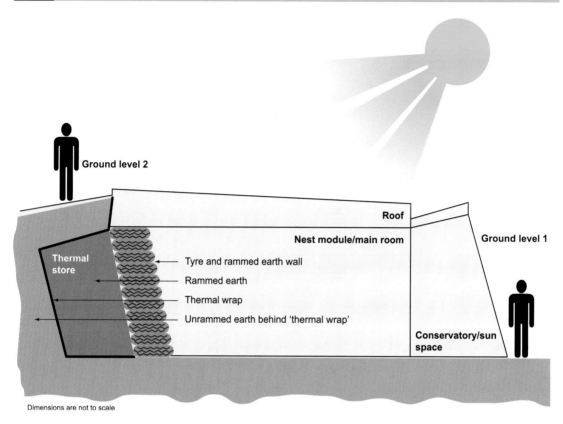

Dimensions are not to scale

Figure 29: Exposure of thermal store at ground level

again reached in March, although the minimum temperature was marginally higher than in 2004.

The evidence suggests that the thermal store is in its charging phase and will continue to do so through future annual cycles, especially after occupation in spring 2007. Monitoring will continue to determine when steady cyclic conditions are achieved.

Temperature gradient in the thermal store (floor upwards)

The average temperatures within the thermal store provide an overall view of when the thermal store is receiving and when it is supplying heat. Further analysis of the individual temperature sensors within the wall demonstrates the pattern of heat storage.

The vertical temperature gradient within the thermal store demonstrates the means by which the thermal store is being charged as seen in Figure 28.

Initial temperatures of all sensors are very similar demonstrating the uniformity of conditions. However, as monitoring progresses during the winter it is the higher points in the thermal store that show

lower temperatures. Further, during the summer months the higher points in the thermal store prove to be higher than the others.

Temperature swings at the top of the thermal store are greater than in other parts, reaching a maximum of over 23°C in September 2005 and a minimum of just below 12°C in March 2006.

These conditions may be explained by the configuration of the thermal store and the internal space, because the earthship is built on a sloping site with the top of the thermal store being ground level at the back of the building and consequently exposed to the external climate (Figure 29). However, the top level of the thermal store is highly insulated and should therefore be largely unaffected by the external climate. The resulting conditions are therefore in need of further investigation.

Horizontal temperature gradient within the tyre wall

The temperature gradient measured by the sensors at different depths away from the wall surface is an

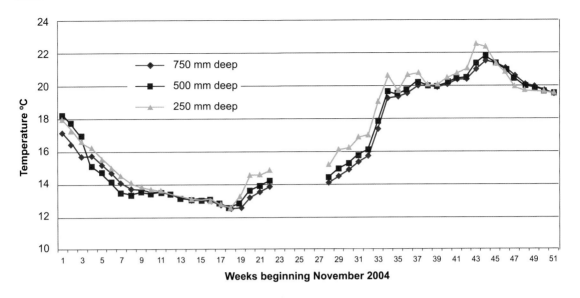

Figure 30: Horizontal temperature gradient in the thermal store

indication of whether heat is flowing into the thermal store from the room or back from the thermal store into the room (Figure 30).

The initial pattern of temperatures gives little indication as both shallow (250 mm) and deep (750 mm) sensors are lower than the one at 500 mm and the relative conditions change until early February when temperatures at all depths are very similar until early spring. At this point there is a clear gradient from shallow to deeper sensors with the temperature nearest the surface being highest and changing more rapidly. The thermal store is therefore charging, with heat being conducted from the higher surface conditions to the lower temperatures within the wall. The current analysis has been based upon weekly average temperatures within the thermal store but further analysis of diurnal fluctuations will give a more detailed understanding of how the thermal store is charging and discharging.

At the beginning of October 2005, the direction of the gradient appears to change, with the shallow temperatures being lower than the deeper ones. Heat is being conducted from the thermal store towards the room in order to maintain stable conditions within the space.

Consideration of stored energy

It has not been possible to evaluate the full extent of the thermal storage as it has only been practical to install sensors up to a depth of 750 mm into the wall and in a limited number of positions. Further, the analysis to date has been based primarily on the sensors buried in the wall to the rear main room.

However, it is reasonable to assume that the results are indicative of conditions within the entire thermal store which wraps around the kitchen, as well as the back and side of the main room. This represents a total volume of 135 m³.

Estimation of the thermal capacity of the wall at this stage is based simply upon published figures for the thermal capacity (1.1 kJ/kg°C) and density (2500 kg/ m³) of chalk.[3.2] It is appreciated that there are risks with using these simple assumptions because of the composite nature of the wall including tyres and chalk, and of the lack of data with respect to the density of compaction or moisture content of the finished wall. However, they enable the order of magnitude of energy storage to be considered.

Energy stored in the tyre wall

Based on the above assumptions, the thermal capacity of a 135 m³ chalk store is 370 MJ °C. Earthship Brighton's thermal store, which showed a 2°C rise over the year of measurement, has therefore captured 740 MJ more than it has released over that time period.

The year of measurement has not been representative of an occupied building as although the envelope was complete the interior has yet to be completed. Thermal conditions within the space have been irregular because the construction has been reliant on voluntary labour and has been intermittent. During construction the building has been subject to doors and windows being left open for long periods.

The continuing monitoring and analysis will include both internal air temperatures and incident solar radiation, but given the unpredictable occupation pattern and level of activity to date it has not yet been considered appropriate to attempt this analysis to date.

Energy flows into the tyre wall

During the weeks from November 2005 through to the end of March 2006 the average temperature of the thermal store dropped steadily by a total of 5°C. This represents a reduction of 1850 MJ. At its peak by mid-September the thermal store temperature had risen 9°C and had therefore taken in 3330 MJ, but by the end of October had dropped 2°C and emitted 740 MJ.

Examination of the temperatures at a depth of 250 mm into the wall shows them to be above the temperatures of the deeper sensors throughout the period when the average temperatures are rising. This demonstrates that the heat energy is flowing into the wall at this stage storing the incident solar radiation and internal gains.

Similarly, thermal store temperatures nearest to the external ground surface show higher temperatures during the summer months reaching a peak in mid-September. After this date the temperatures drop and reach the same temperature as the sensor 630 mm deeper below the surface level by early November.

an occupied building; however the results clearly indicate the nature of energy flows to and from the thermal store.

The next stage in the analysis is to evaluate energy flows accounting for the external climate conditions including incident solar radiation and the temperatures within the occupied space. Monitoring will continue at least until steady cyclic conditions are achieved within the thermal store and an assessment of whether additional winter heating will be required for an occupied building.

Development is also in progress to produce a computerised thermal model of an earth sheltered building in order to enable further analysis and optimisation of the thermal capacity and heat transfer properties of the thermal store.

ACKNOWLEDGEMENTS

We are grateful to the EU Interreg programme for the funding of the project which undertook 12 case studies of which the earthship was one. We thank the members of the Durabuild team, Kenneth Ip, Kath Shaw and Marta Lam and the Low Carbon Trust, especially Mischa Hewitt the project manager, for their contributions to the research.

REFERENCES AND NOTES

[3.1] Carbon Trust (2006). The carbon emissions generated in all that we consume.

[3.2] ArupGeotechnics (2002). Ground storage of building heat energy: overview report O-02-ARUP3, DTI Partners in Innovation.

CONCLUSION

Earthship Brighton has provided the Centre for Sustainability of the Built Environment at the University of Brighton the opportunity to gain real time measurements within the thermal store of a building designed on the principles of 'glass and mass'. The unfinished nature of the building has meant that the results are not representative of

*Photovoltaic cells at the
Hockerton Housing Project*

CHAPTER 4
RENEWABLE ENERGY

INTRODUCTION

Earthships cannot do the main thing that we expect of most ships – moving from place to place. However, the obvious similarity to sailing ships is that they also directly employ the natural phenomena they encounter to their advantage. So the analogy of a yacht or sailing ship – a human construction that uses renewable natural resources (the wind, tide and currents) to effortlessly achieve its goals of travelling from one place to another seems an appropriate one. This is especially the case when we consider the 'freedom' of the ship to travel using only these abundant, renewable and free natural resources without recourse to non-sustainable fuels. The earthship is similarly unconstrained as it is designed to be unconnected to the national grid or other utilities. The aim of the earthship is to provide comfortable shelter for its inhabitants through a set of sustainable means analogous to those of a sailing boat, though the 'wind in the sails' of the earthship is not for movement but for providing space heating through thermal mass and the energy generation to power the systems required for human habitation.

Figure 31: Earthship Brighton showing a wind turbine, photovoltaic cells and solar thermal panels

The word 'earthship' might also be familiar from the term 'Spaceship Earth', coined by engineer, architect and innovator R Buckminster Fuller.[4.1] This concept states that our planet itself can be seen as a ship that is travelling through space powered by the sun and capable of constantly regenerating life. Earthships could be seen as a microscopic expression of this belief as they are also fundamentally powered by the sun and are analogous to a ship in the ways we have discussed above.

This chapter looks at the specific energy strategies used by earthships, and particularly how they derive electrical energy from site-available resources. This is also part of a more general look at how UK housing might turn from its present dependence on unsustainable and carbon emissions-heavy energy sources to a sustainable low carbon future. This in turn is influenced by the energy market in general and so we briefly look at some possible future alternatives for long term energy strategy in the UK. We recognise that there is a lot of ground to cover on this subject and this chapter cannot hope to cover all of it. However, it does constitute an attempt to put the renewable energy strategies of earthships into the fullest possible context of the future of renewable energy in general in the UK.

OFFGRID CONSTRUCTION

In a relatively small and developed country such as the UK there is presently little direct need for offgrid construction due to the extensive infrastructure that supplies the majority of demand in the country. Only in the most remote settlements is there a need for buildings to be offgrid and therefore the demand for autonomous homes is not a large scale movement or part of a government strategy. So why is the offgrid approach being adopted with earthships? There are a number of reasons, but perhaps the primary one is that the philosophy of these buildings is about complete self-sufficiency and connection to outside utilities of any sort is essentially an admission of non-self sufficiency. Earthships only use the resources that are immediately available to them thereby not extending the footprint of the building beyond its means. By contrast, homes that require utilities to be piped and wired in to them in order to comfortably accommodate people, could be seen as fundamentally failing to deliver their most basic aim:

to provide safe and comfortable shelter. In the event of any kind of breakdown of utilities, this ability is severely compromised.

But for all this to really make sense, it needs to be related to the wider picture of energy use in the UK. It is important to emphasise the fact that electrical energy forms only a third of the UK's total energy use, with heat energy also constituting a third and transport the final third, so the emphasis should not rest entirely on electricity generation as is sometimes seen to be the case. And the core question that needs to be asked is: what is the best and most practicable route for major reductions in all building-related carbon emissions? Is it through enormous investment in grid based renewable solutions or through mass devolvement of generation to the scale of individual dwelling microgeneration and multi-dwelling microgeneration on private wire grids such as Hockerton, BedZED and Findhorn? Or is the solution to be found through a combination of these means? All the solutions have to be building-focused in terms of measures to improve efficiency and slash demand before consideration of how different supply options can provide clean and zero carbon energy to those homes. We will look at how earthships feed in to some of these ideas by first of all considering an outline government position and some precedents for sustainable energy strategies already in existence in UK buildings.

LOW ENERGY FUTURE – THE CONTEMPORARY UK SITUATION

In its vision of the future of energy set out in the 2003 *Energy white paper*,[4.2] and subsequently endorsed in the 2006 *Energy review*,[4.3] the Department of Trade and Industry (DTI) endorses trailblazing constructions with low grid demand and the capability to sell excess electricity back to the network, by predicting that this approach will be widespread within the next 15 years. By 2020, the *Energy white paper* says:

"New homes will be designed to need very little energy and will perhaps even achieve zero carbon emissions. The existing building stock will increasingly adopt energy efficient measures. Many buildings will have the capacity at least to reduce their demand on the grid, for example by using solar heating systems to provide some of their water heating needs, if not to generate electricity to sell back into the local network."[4.2]

This statement of intent from 2003 achieved greater significance and more bite in 2006 with the advent of the Code for Sustainable Homes,[4.4] the first step in a series of measures to ensure that all new houses built after 2016 are zero carbon homes (see Box 3 in chapter 1: Defining a zero carbon home). The government statement in 2006 said that "energy efficient and insulated buildings, which draw their energy from zero or low carbon technologies and therefore produce no net carbon emissions from all energy use over the course of a year, will help reduce carbon emissions as well as lowering fuel bills for households".[4.3]

Although there are precedents for low grid demand developments, including BedZED in south London (Figure 32), Robert and Brenda Vale's Hockerton Housing Project in Nottinghamshire, and Findhorn eco-village in Scotland, totally off-grid constructions

with renewable energy sources remain confined to a very limited number of small developments, including the two earthships presently in existence in the UK. The 'ZED' of BedZED stands for 'Zero Energy Development' and it uses many of the similar principles of energy-conscious design as earthships: passive solar, thermal mass, super insulation and passive ventilation, to achieve its stated goal. As observed with earthships, this cuts direct energy requirements enormously and makes it far easier to fill the 'energy gap' with renewable sources – in the case of BedZED a combined heat and power (CHP) plant and photovoltaic cells. When excess amounts of electricity are produced, they can then be sold back to the network. However, BedZED is unable to be totally self-sufficient in terms of energy needs the whole time; at certain peak periods of high demand, such as between 4 and 7pm in winter months, it has to import electricity from the grid to cover the energy deficit.[4.5] The surplus for export back into the grid will be made in the summer and results in a

Figure 32: BedZED uses a combined heat and power plant and photovoltaic cells

net-zero carbon result over a typical year according to BedZED itself. Significantly, though, it is only able to achieve this through connection with the grid.

There is evidence that households that start using microgeneration immediately cut their energy consumption, as demonstrated by a recent study by the Sustainable Consumption Roundtable.[4.6] Schemes championing microgeneration are gaining widespread recognition in the UK, including earthships, the Hockerton Housing Project, the Oxford Eco House and a number of projects in London backed by the London Climate Change Agency (LCCA) such as Palestra in London SE1. LCCA is committed to 'a high decentralised energy scenario' for London from 2005 to 2025, ensuring local security of supply through promotion of small scale renewable generated CHP networks providing virtual self-sufficiency from the grid for communities on their own 'private wire networks' based on evolving hydrogen technologies.[4.7] However, there remains significant scepticism about the effect microgeneration can have in terms of its impact on the energy mix and the overall reduction of carbon emissions into the atmosphere.

But the adherents of microgeneration (such as architect Bill Dunster, whose company designed BedZED and a number of other zero emission, zero carbon developments with photovoltaics and microwind technology) suggest that the combination of new build and retrofitting with increased energy efficiency and virtually self-sufficient microgenerative capacity are absolutely essential to the UK's energy strategy. Bill Dunster says that "The only way of living in a low-carbon future is to reduce demand by 80% and then microgenerate the remaining 20% with building integrated renewable technologies. This leaves scarce green grid electricity for public transport, heritage buildings, industry and food production/distribution."[4.5] In an attempt to roll out low carbon living to a mass market, Bill Dunster's architectural practice ZED Factory developed a relatively inexpensive kit house called RuralZED for which wind and photovoltaic microgeneration could each provide up to 50% of the total electricity demand for each building. Water heating is provided by a biomass boiler and solar thermal heater.

There is a widespread consensus that there will be an increasingly heterogeneous and decentralised energy market in the medium term future, with renewables occupying a larger share of a growing market (total energy use is predicted to continue rising indefinitely in the short to medium term). The government envisages that by 2020, 20% of total UK grid electricity will be derived from renewable sources, particularly large scale wind farms.[4.3] But this heterogeneous energy market will also continue to include nuclear energy and fossil fuels for many years. Indeed, some commentators predict that gas fired power may have a greater than 50% share of the market beyond 2020.[4.8]

Energy companies do realise that there is an increasing consumer demand for carbon neutral energy, and there are a number of schemes that allow customers to get their electricity supplied on a 'green tariff' that is specifically linked to renewables generation eg NPower's Juice tariff.[4.9] These tariffs operate on the principle of displacement, as once generated power is on the network there is no sense of differentiation as to the origin of that power. So buyers are purchasing electricity that has effectively been generated from the same multiplicity of sources as exist throughout the country, although their payment is mainly directed to specifically identified renewable generators. But consumers of these tariffs are also covering centralised costs – and creating profit – for companies such as NPower who continue to promote the use of fossil fuel generation as their core business. Therefore, it is certainly arguable that there is no pure sense in which the consumer can ever be entirely carbon neutral in their electricity usage while remaining on the grid unless they have zero or negative (ie they generate enough net electricity to sell back to the network) consumption.

Perhaps the key argument, though, is that fundamentally inefficient national grid linked homes, on green tariffs or not, have little impulse to decrease their demand, which is the vital first step for any major reduction in carbon emissions. This could have a great deal to do with the 'disassociation' of behaviour with environmental impacts, part of the general alienation of people from their natural environment. Microgeneration, by contrast, bridges the gap between people and the natural world by making manifest the essential connection of natural resources to the viability of human life.

LARGE SCALE INFRASTRUCTURE AND ITS CARBON IMPLICATIONS

The fact that earthships found their genesis in extraordinarily remote places created a genuine need for this self-sufficiency, but that does not diminish their value in a setting where infrastructure does exist. By making use of natural resources to power the earthship, it means that no more energy is ever used than is immediately available to the building. At the moment, the only real restriction in general energy usage is the ability of the buyer to afford it, which encourages non-sustainable levels of consumption powered by finite fossil fuel reserves, which currently provide more than 70% of UK grid electricity (renewables provide approximately 4% and the government target is for this figure to reach 10% by 2010 under the Renewable Energy Obligation).[4.8]

The national grid is not a storage mechanism but a network of delivery for electricity, although it does have some very limited storage capacity within it. However, the fundamental principle of the grid is that it fills real time demand for electricity with real time generation and supply. The main challenge for an offgrid building such as the earthship, therefore, is to achieve exactly what the grid does – to match its ability to generate and supply electricity to the demand at any given time. Earthships, though, have nowhere to import electricity from if there is a deficit situation. Instead, they compensate for the likely potential of deficit by using deep cycle lead acid storage batteries. Therefore surplus energy can be stored from peak periods of production to be used at a later time. However, this is a somewhat controversial approach due to the limited longevity of lead acid batteries and the fact that lead is an exceptionally toxic manufacturing process ie some poisonous waste is created via this approach (Figure 33). But batteries could be considered as a 'transitional technology' with more sophisticated technologies for energy storage under development. If a cleaner alternative for lead acid batteries could be found then there are very few down sides to the offgrid earthship model.

There are significant problems associated with integration with the grid, particularly in terms of efficiency and reliability. The grid is an inefficient system that, according to Ofgem, loses 9% of its total energy through transmission and distribution alone.[4.7] More than 90% of the gross amount of energy on the grid is also supplied by power stations that have a thermal efficiency of less than 50%.[4.10] And in terms of billing, there is a highly complex set of costs that are added to each basic unit of electricity and passed on to the consumer, including VAT, climate change levy, renewable obligation and distribution and transmission losses. This means that the consumer is paying more than four times the wholesale price for their power, but if they generate enough energy to sell back to the network they would not get any more than the basic wholesale price.

In terms of reliability, or what in the energy industry is usually called 'security of supply' there are many factors that might jeopardise the delivery of gas and electricity through the grid:

- Extreme weather conditions leading to infrastructure problems – through high winds and flooding for example – and failure of supply to meet demand, as happened in certain areas of London in July 2006 when enormous demand from air conditioning and refrigeration units led to power cuts.

Figure 33: Trojan batteries before installation (Earthship Brighton)

- The massive increase in costs that make energy unaffordable such as the 58% net increase in electricity prices across the UK between January 2003 and October 2004.
- The possibility of even greater price volatility based on 'peak oil' theories about diminishing fossil fuel reserves.
- Political instability, terrorism and computer malfunction.

The consideration of all these factors starts to make offgrid living a very attractive proposition. It means that householders have control over their ability to maintain a comfortable standard of living, without needing to worry about a number of things that could have an adverse effect if the home was on the grid.

In an era where 'risk management' is so ubiquitous, the concepts of offgrid living, self-sufficiency and autonomy seem entirely appropriate reactions to many of the challenges faced in 21st Century society. In the energy industry, security of supply is, as might be expected, one of the primary requirements of any energy source. Renewable offgrid living means that householders have control of and responsibility for their own energy supply. As long as the

Table 5: System sizing spreadsheet for Earthship Brighton

Outgoing energy

Device	Voltage	Wattage	Current	Hours/day summer	Hours/day winter	Inverter efficiency	Total daily summer (Ah)	Total daily winter (Ah)
DC loads								
Fridge	24.00	140.00	5.83	18.00	12.00	n/a	105.00	70.00
Pump	24.00	6.00	0.25	8.00	8.00	n/a	2.00	2.00
Pump	24.00	6.00	0.25	8.00	8.00	n/a	2.00	2.00
AC loads								
Laptop	24.00	30.00	1.25	8.00	8.00	0.90	11.11	11.11
Laptop	24.00	30.00	1.25	8.00	8.00	0.90	11.11	11.11
Laptop	24.00	30.00	1.25	8.00	8.00	0.90	11.11	11.11
Printer ink jet	24.00	50.00	2.08	4.00	4.00	0.90	9.26	9.26
Projector	24.00	800.00	33.33	1.00	1.00	0.90	37.04	37.04
Stereo	24.00	75.00	3.13	4.00	4.00	0.90	13.89	13.89
						Totals (Ah/day)	202.52	167.52

Incoming energy

Device	Voltage	Wattage	Current	Hours/day summer	Hours/day winter	Inverter efficiency	Total daily summer (Ah)	Total daily winter (Ah)
18 × 62 W Unisolar electric panels	24.00	1116.00	46.5	6.00	–	3.00	279.00	139.50
900 W Whisper H40 wind turbine	24.00	900.00	37.5	2.00	–	4.00	75.00	150.00
						Totals (Ah/day)	354.00	289.50
						Ah: Available excess energy	151.48	121.98

technology is reliable, then, this ensures security of supply but also less severe consequences in the event of technological failure as offgrid buildings need to be designed to use as little energy as possible. Earthships are therefore better equipped to deal with a temporary lack of electrical input than conventional housing.

ENERGY DEMAND MANAGEMENT IN EARTHSHIPS

The earthship's energy strategy is two fold – firstly in terms of energy conscious design that reduces the need for external energy inputs of any sort, even those of a sustainable kind; and secondly in terms of the actual microrenewable energy generation systems that provide electricity and hot water to the building. This can be thought of as supply and demand: the first step is to slash energy demand so that the second step can be easily met with renewable sources. A process of 'system sizing' – evaluating the capacity requirements of an earthship and integrating the correct level of supply to meet those requirements – needs to take place in order to 'balance the books'. The system sizing spreadsheet for Earthship Brighton is included in Table 5 for reference. Note how the supply side is much greater than the demand side. This 'over capacity' is essential due to the fact that the microgenerative technologies in use – wind and solar – are weather dependent and may not produce the peak outputs they are capable of.

Not only is the design energy conscious, but to a certain degree it also has to rely on the conscientiousness of the occupants to use energy frugally. With an offgrid building like this it has to be a case of tailoring activities and using any excess power at any given time. Indeed, there is a demand from earthships that profligate and wasteful consumption of energy is a thing of the past – a general idea that on one hand seems to be gaining increasingly widespread acceptance across the UK.[4.11] Of course on the other hand there is an increasing demand for energy hungry air conditioning units and a proliferation of electronic devices and gadgets acting to balance out this energy saving impulse and maintain the overall upwards trend of electricity consumption.

The significant point is that comfortable living, low carbon living in luxury, is made easy in earthships without resorting to the high energy usage seen in the vast majority of the present UK building stock, where demands for basic services such as space heating on their own represent a massive drain on the grid due predominantly to poor design. And that is before assessing the impact of an arsenal of modern appliances: water heating, TV, computers and other gadgets.

The combined passive solar and thermal mass capacity of earthships is the most critical factor in reducing energy requirements for the building. This is not only in terms of the more obvious reduction in space heating requirement, but also in terms of lighting, which is seldom necessary during daylight hours due to the enormous amount of south facing glazing in the building and despite the fact that the rear of the building is bermed into the earth (skylights compensate for the lack of north facing windows). But the fact that earthships allow light to flood into them is also emblematic of the primacy of the sun in their overall design. It is true to say that earthships, in the most direct way, are powered by the sun and many design features, from the building's orientation to thermal mass, large glazing area to water recycling, are all solar oriented. The building itself is like a rechargeable battery that uses the sun to keep it charged and functioning, while collecting and using as much solar energy as possible through various means.

HARVESTING PASSIVE SOLAR ENERGY

The two principal means by which solar energy is used by the earthship are through solar thermal collection – both passive solar and solar water heating – and electricity generation. According to Bob Everett, a 'perfectly ordinary' badly insulated 1970s UK house is already 14% passive solar heated in terms of the sun's contribution to the gross annual heating demand of the building.[4.12] However, the remaining 86% net space heating demand will need to be supplied from fossil fuel sources – either gas or electricity from the grid – on average between mid-September and mid-May. The earthship, on the other hand, tries to achieve a 100% contribution to gross heating demand from passive solar input throughout the year, requiring zero, or negligible, additional heating.

Mike Reynolds states that "heating and cooling ie maintaining temperatures near to their accepted comfort zone, are inherent qualities of earthship design. Initial design of the earthship allows the natural phenomenon of thermal mass to prevail and presents the reality of avoiding (the necessity of having) a heating or cooling system of any kind."[4.13]

While this has been reviewed in detail in chapter 3, it is important to recognise how this strategy impacts on the amount of energy generation that needs to take place to make the earthship a comfortable structure for human habitation. Cutting energy demand is the first step to achieving a zero carbon solution. Without having yet looked at microrenewable electrical generation then, it is clear that the earthship effectively uses solar energy to enormously reduce further energy demands. This technique in itself is far from unique but it is stretched to a particularly extreme level in the case of earthships, which makes the prospect of a totally offgrid building a far more realistic proposition.

Microgeneration is likely to struggle to make a significant impact on building stock where 57% of the total energy demand is represented by a space heating requirement. Present technologies on a domestic scale are simply incapable of providing the level of demand that these fundamentally inefficient dwellings require. It has been estimated that at the present rate of demolition, it would take approximately 886 years to replace the entire UK building stock, so it is clear that new build can only have a very limited impact in adding low carbon, microgenerative homes, assuming that all new build fits that bill, which it clearly will not do for many years.[4.14] In fact the net size of the UK building stock is estimated to increase by at least 2 million homes by 2020, which, in itself, will result in an overall increase of 8 million tonnes of carbon emissions a year, based on the government target of a 20% emissions reduction being achieved.[4.9] Extensive retrofitting of the existing stock with a number of measures predominantly to improve heat efficiency coupled with microgeneration could be a solution that overcomes this ponderous pace of change: but there are significant barriers to this, predominantly due to the fact that the burden of cost is placed firmly with individual householders. Significant fiscal initiatives from government would be needed to improve domestic energy efficiency and increase rates of deployment for microgenerative technology.

MICRORENEWABLE SYSTEMS

Wind power

Power derived from wind has been used by mankind for many centuries for applications such as milling grain and pumping water, though it has only relatively recently been used as a source of electricity. At present, wind is still the most cost effective source of generating renewable electricity. Turbines are capable of being installed in any location where there is a reasonable amount of wind; average UK sources suggest between 4 and 10 m/s and the units are nominally rated at 1 kW at a given wind speed of 12 m/s (Figure 34).

Figure 34: Whisper wind turbine (Earthship Brighton)

Small wind turbine generating systems are products which are environmentally friendly renewable energy devices that are 'wind operated' and generate electricity that is synchronous with mains supply. The electricity generated is 'plugged in' to the building's standard ring mains supply for 230 V AC, 50 Hz applications. The wind turbine units are also referred to as small scale embedded generators.

Photovoltaics

Photovoltaic solar power is one of the most promising of renewable energy sources as the technology does not pollute the environment and the sun is a virtually infinite source of energy (Figures 35, 37 and 38). Indeed, as Godfrey Boyle has pointed out, the net solar power input to the earth is more than 10 000 times humanity's current rate of use of fossil and nuclear fuels.

Photovoltaic cells convert sunlight into electricity. Solar cells work in both types of light: diffuse light through clouds (no direct sunshine) and direct light (sunshine) to convert light into electricity. Direct sunlight produces the most energy although the efficiency can vary greatly depending on the type of photovoltaic cell: monocrystalline, polycrystalline or amorphous silicon.

Earthship Brighton uses 18, 62 W Unisolar electric panels while Earthship Fife uses four BP275F 75 W monocrystalline solar panels (see Table 6 for details).

Figure 35: Filsol solar thermal panels (Earthship Brighton)

Figure 36: Installing whisper wind turbine (Earthship Brighton)

Solar thermal – domestic water heating

Solar thermal is a highly viable and relatively simple technology that can be used to supply hot water for domestic applications such as dishwashing and showers. This type of use accounted for approximately 7% of the total national energy use in the UK in 2000. Bob Everett says that "domestic water heating is perhaps the best overall potential application for active solar heating in Europe".[4.12] According to him, domestic water heating uses approximately 15 kWh per day in a typical UK household and much of this energy will be lost as waste heat.

The problem in the UK, however, is the paucity of sunshine hours in the winter, which makes solar thermal a seasonally restrictive technology. However, as hot water is in demand throughout the year (as opposed to space heating, for which there is little demand in the UK summer), it means that it can make a significant contribution to overall energy demand.

Earthship Brighton uses two 2 m² Filsol solar thermal panels.

Bioenergy or biomass

Bioenergy refers to energy derived from fuels that were, until recently, alive. This normally means materials such as wood and straw. By burning this biomass it is possible to obtain electricity using a similar methodology as would be used with fossil fuels such as coal. However, the difference is that whereas coal is a finite resource, biomass renews itself again and again as long as the correct

Figure 37 (left): Photovoltaic panels at the Eden Project

Figure 38 (below): Filsol solar thermal panels and Unisolar photovoltaic panels (Earthship Brighton)

conditions are provided for it to do so. Biomass has a crucial interdependence with the atmosphere and plants are responsible for generating oxygen and 'fixing' atmospheric CO_2. The crucial aspect of the use of biomass, though, is that "provided our consumption does not exceed the natural level of production, the combustion of biofuels should generate no more heat and create no more CO_2 than would have been formed in any case by natural processes".[4.12] Thus there is the opportunity for sustainable production of biomass as purpose-grown energy crops, providing a truly sustainable energy source. There are problems with bioenergy – such as the amount of land it requires for the energy return and transport implications for example – but it is nonetheless a promising form of renewable energy that can be used effectively as a microgenerative technique.

Earthship Brighton uses a 15 kW Extraflame wood pellet stove that uses wood pellets produced from sustainable sources (Figure 39).

Figure 39: Extraflame wood pellet stove (Earthship Brighton)

Microhydro

Hydroelectricity on a mass scale is already an enormously successful form of renewable energy, providing as it does about a sixth of the world's annual electrical output and over 90% of electricity from renewables.[4.12] Of course, it is a far less universal resource than sunlight and wind, and not every site will be able to use this form of generation. However, the point is about site harmony and opportunism: using the resources that are available to contribute to the overall demand. Earthship Fife uses a microhydro turbine that runs in an onsite stream (Figure 40).

Figure 40: Turgo Runner Stream Engine microhydro turbine (Earthship Fife)

FINANCIAL IMPLICATIONS OF OFFGRID LIVING

There is a significant positive cost implication of being offgrid that is a further argument in favour of offgrid microgeneration. A single upfront capital expense upon construction means that the building will run on a lifelong perpetual 'income' of natural resources that cuts out utility bills entirely, whether they rise exponentially or not. Mike Reynolds estimates that earthships require, on average, a 10% greater initial capital investment than a conventional

Table 6: Earthship Brighton and Earthship Fife power generation systems specification

Technology	Purpose	Earthship Brighton	Earthship Fife
Photovoltaic	Electricity	18 x 62 W Unisolar electric panels	4 x BP275F 75 W monocrystalline solar panels
Capacity	–	1.116 kW	300 W
Wind turbine	Electricity	900 W Whisper H40 wind turbine	Proven WT600 W
Microhydro	Electricity	–	1 kW Turgo Runner Stream Engine
Total peak capacity	–	2 kW	1.9 kW
Solar thermal	Water heating	2 x 2 m² Filsol panels	–
Anticipated yield	–	1636 kWh	–
Biomass: wood pellet	Water heating	15 kW Extraflame wood pellet stove	–
Anticipated yield	–	Varies depending on use	–

Table 7: Earthship Brighton and Earthship Fife power systems capital costs

Technology	Earthship Brighton	Earthship Fife
Photovoltaic and equipment	£6760.95	£1300.00
Wind turbine and equipment	£4660.64	£4265.00
Microhydro and equipment	–	£2500.00
Power organising module*	£3000.00	£3344.00
Batteries	£7435.40	£1250.00
Solar thermal	£3732.75	–
Biomass: wood pellet	£3072.74	–
Total	£28 662.48	£12 659.00

All figures include VAT
*Includes charge controller, inverter and fusebox.

Table 8: Earthship Brighton and Earthship Fife power systems control batteries

Earthship	Earthship Brighton	Earthship Fife
Batteries	40 x Trojan deep cycle lead acid	12 x deep cycle lead acid
Voltage	24 V	24 V
Storage capacity	46 kWh	18 kWh

home in order to realise this possibility.[4.15] In a time of instability in energy prices, which has seen large price rises for provision of gas and electricity in the UK, this is an envious financial position for the offgrid householder to be in. It also adds a further tier to the concept of freedom that the earthship embodies – freedom from regular utility bills is something that most people in the developed world would like to achieve.

Mike Reynolds also sees offgrid living as a way in which people can rapidly evolve more appropriate systems to face numerous environmental and structural challenges whereas centralised infrastructure remains sluggishly slow to evolve. "Decentralised utilities can completely eliminate the expensive and invasive web of wires and pipes that currently deliver centralized utilities," says Mike Reynolds. "Both the manufacture and delivery

Figure 41: A power organising module: controller, inverter and fusebox (Earthship Brighton)

of centralized utilities put individual people in a powerless and vulnerable position with respect to security and evolution."[4.15]

The technology that enables individuals to escape from the 'invasive web of wires' that Mike Reynolds describes is microrenewable power, mainly in the form of photovoltaic generation and microwind turbines, as described in brief above. The electrical supply in earthships is regulated by a power organising module which consists of a change controller, inverter and fusebox (Figure 41). The government has made significant claims to be supporting microgenerative technologies in the UK in a number of papers including the 2003 *Energy white paper*[4.2] and the 2006 *Energy review*[4.3] and the DTI commissioned Energy Saving Trust report estimated that microgeneration could reduce household carbon emissions by 15%. December 2006 saw the Barker review on planning commissioned by the treasury make a number of recommendations to make the planning process easier for potential domestic and commercial microgeneration projects through changes to Planning Policy Statement 22: *Renewable energy*.[4.16] But the £133 million of government money over the last few years that has

been allocated to the promotion of microgeneration is seen by many as a derisory sum (it has been described as 'woefully inadequate' by the chief executive of the Redevelopment Energy Association, for example).[4.10]

That level of fiscal commitment would seem to be a direct reflection of the minor role the government actually sees microgeneration making to the overall energy mix. Microgeneration is realistically seen as a way in which the gross national energy demand can be held in check somewhat. Present models see overall energy demand maintaining a steady increase and creating a gap between generation and demand potential unless major new generation comes on tap in the medium term. If the UK government delivers on its aspirations as set out in the 2006 *Energy review*[4.3] then renewables will form a much bigger part of this ultimate generation mix as long as demand does not massively increase. This is significant due to the fact that renewables technology will not be able to be deployed quickly enough to respond to a massive increase in demand and other alternatives that use widely deployed existing technologies will have to fill the gap that renewables are unable to fill. The promotion of widespread energy efficiency and mass microgeneration are potentially significant factors in achieving this goal of stemming the tide of energy demand, which makes government efforts to date in terms of funding seem baffling.

The earthship is a pragmatic building, dictated by function. It is therefore open to any renewable form of microgeneration to fill its energy demands. At Earthship Fife this takes the form three different types of technology: a photovoltaic array, a wind turbine and a hydro turbine. Earthship Brighton uses only a photovoltaic array and wind turbine. Tables 7 and 8 specify exactly what is being used in both projects.

CONCLUSION

Earthships are exemplars of good practice in terms of the standardised energy hierarchy: they focus on energy efficiency and reducing demand first of all before seeking to supply capacity requirements from renewable sources. This is key to the overall energy strategy of the buildings and constitutes the most fundamental requirement for all zero carbon homes.

The real essence of earthships is in harnessing renewable natural resources not just for electricity generation but also for passive space heating and ventilation, lighting and water heating. By using these site available resources, earthships are able to be offgrid and detached from all the problems that are part and parcel of centralised infrastructure. It also means that it is virtually impossible to have a net carbon footprint, unlike buildings that are connected to the grid – limited capacity enforces responsible, energy wise behaviour. This is achieved not only through limited capacity, though, but also due to householders achieving increased connectivity on a psychological level with their natural environment. This means that they control their own means of electrical production and clearly see the link between natural resources and the power required to run their home. The 2005 Sustainable Development Commission paper on microgeneration said that: "Beyond the sheer excitement and pleasure of DIY electricity generation, the impact is seen in householders' shifting attitudes to energy conservation and consumption."[4.6]

The potential problem of a supply deficit is compensated for by storage batteries and an over capacity of supply that is integrated during the formative stages of system sizing. There are negative implications with batteries, but they should be balanced against the benefits that earthships offer in general and the many negative aspects of centralised infrastructure. There is also the possibility of supply failure, despite the techniques that are employed to prevent that eventuality. This is both unlikely and would also have less problematic consequences than a breakdown in a conventional infrastructure-dependent home where fewer services are embedded within the building fabric itself.

Earthships are pioneers of what can be achieved through microgeneration and show that non-grid based solutions are viable on a single dwelling basis. The government's definition of a zero carbon home (see Box 3 in Chapter 1) Defining a zero carbon home) supports the notion that onsite generation – either at a single dwelling or on a developmental level – is a key criterion, rather than relying on imported electricity. Trying to build as much self-sufficiency into new build as possible in the UK is essential to try and wean buildings from a paradigmatically flawed reliance on centralised infrastructure. The earthship shows how basic resources can provide all the energy that is needed,

when generative techniques are integrated into a successful design. It is clear that more fiscal incentives are needed to encourage microgeneration to make a meaningful impact on overall domestic carbon emissions. However, major new development projects such as at Middlehaven in Middlesborough and Gallions Park in London look set to start providing new models of microgeneration at a developmental level.

However, it is more difficult to effectively and meaningfully retrofit microgenerative technologies into the existing inefficient building stock; that is where major capacity increases are necessary in supplying grid-based renewable power in order to provide greater sustainability and less carbon emissions across the board. Microgeneration and small scale networks in a devolved energy strategy may be the long term future that has to be invested in now in terms of new build. But grid-based renewable generation to power the inefficient building stock seems essential for the short and medium term.

REFERENCES AND NOTES

[4.1] R Buckminster Fuller (1976). Operating manual for spaceship earth. New York, Aenonian Press.

[4.2] DTI (2003). Energy white paper.

[4.3] DCLG (2006). Energy review.

[4.4] DCLG (2006) The code for sustainable homes.

[4.5] Dunster B (2006). From A to ZED: Realising zero (fossil) energy developments. (2nd ed). Wallington, Surrey, ZED Factory Ltd.

[4.6] Sustainable Consumption Roundtable (2005). Seeing the light: the impact of microgeneration on the way we use energy – qualitative research findings. Written and researched by The Hub Research Consultants on behalf of the Sustainable Consumption Roundtable. Download from www.sd-commission.org.uk.

[4.7] LCCA. Presentation by Allan Jones, chief executive officer, London Climate Change Agency: Urban change on a large-scale at: Renewable energy in the new low carbon Britain: 2020 and beyond. A conference hosted by the Energy Institute, 5 December 2006.

[4.8] Poyry Consulting. Presentation by Richard Slark: The role of renewables in the UK generation mix: independent forecasts for 2010, 2015 and 2020 at Renewable energy in the new low carbon Britain: 2020 and beyond. A conference hosted by the Energy Institute, 5 December 2006.

[4.9] NPower. Presentation by Robert Harper, product manager. Environment and renewables: NPower proceedings at Renewable energy in the new low carbon Britain: 2020 and beyond. A conference hosted by the Energy Institute, 5 December 2006.

[4.10] Renewable Energy Association. Presentation by Philip Wolfe, chief executive officer at Renewable energy in the new low carbon Britain: 2020 and beyond. A conference hosted by the Energy Institute, 5 December 2006.

[4.11] See the BBC website, for example, which offers numerous tips on saving energy in the home: http://news.bbc.co.uk/1/hi/uk/6076658.stm.

[4.12] Boyle G (ed) (2004). Renewable energy. Oxford, Oxford University Press, p31.

[4.13] Reynolds M (1990). Earthship Volume 1: How to build your own. Taos, New Mexico, Solar Survival Press.

[4.14] ODPM (2005). ODPM statistical release 2006/0042.

[4.15] Reynolds M (2006). A presentation to Green Party councillors at Brighton Town Hall on June 26, 2006; also conversations with the authors.

[4.16] DCLG (2004). Planning Policy Statement 22: Renewable energy.

Rainwater harvesting system in action at the Eden Project's 'core' building.

CHAPTER 5
WATER

INTRODUCTION

The UK is famous for its changeable weather, come fair, foul, rain or shine. This green and pleasant land, the 'emerald isle', receives on average over 1 m of rain per year (Figure 42 illustrates the average rainfall distribution). Yet the country emerged in winter 2006/07 from one of the longest periods of sustained drought in the last 100 years.[5.1] Caught between the creaking leaking pipes and one of the highest uses per head in Europe, certain parts of the UK are now at crisis point, with the groundwater at a historic low and further depletion taking place each year. Of all the water on earth, only 1% is fresh water and within this only 1% is suitable for human consumption; the rest is either locked up in ice caps or is inaccessible. Water is one of the most precious natural resources and earthships, through harvesting and recycling of rainwater, demonstrates a solution without the need to draw water from the ground or rivers, enabling us to conserve fresh water reserves and the environment they support. This chapter is about the earthship water systems and starts by setting them in the context of the current UK water situation by looking at rainfall, large scale distribution and levels of domestic demand. After a brief discussion of alternative water sources, the earthship rainwater harvesting, grey and blackwater recycling systems are explored in detail, with particular reference to Earthship Brighton and Earthship Fife.

LARGE SCALE WATER DISTRIBUTION UNDER PRESSURE

The contemporary situation

Water is essential for life and the supply of it in any country relies on the delicate balance of a number of factors, from how much rain there is, the level of infrastructure in place to collect, treat and distribute it, and finally the number of people and settlements that consume it. Any imbalance in this complex dynamic can lead to a water shortage or drought and these are not rare occurrences: there have been 10 severe droughts in the last 100 years, with several lasting two years or more, such as the 1933/4, 1975/6 and 1989/90 droughts.[5.2] From a point of view of water, England and Wales are divided up into various regions between 25 water companies who apply for licences from the Environment Agency to abstract water from rivers and groundwater aquifers, which is then sold to their customers. This has been the situation since the Water Act controversially privatised water in 1989. The situation is the same in Scotland, while in Northern Ireland the water supplies are still publicly owned.

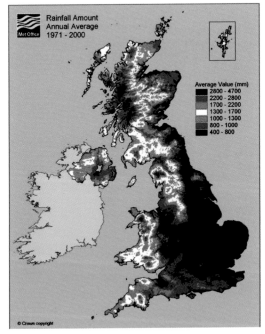

Figure 42: UK average annual rainfall distribution. Source: Met Office Crown Copyright 2007

demonstrate that they are persuading their domestic and commercial customers to introduce a raft of water conservation measures before they are allowed to apply to abstract more water from rivers, as was the case in winter 2006. Such a decision was made by the Department for Food and Rural Affairs (DEFRA) to allow permits for the increased removal of water from the hydrological cycle. This had dire consequences for the rivers and eco-systems dependent on the water whose needs are being placed behind that of people. The environment minister, Elliot Morley, in a written ministerial statement was forced to conclude that "In many parts of the country, water is a precious resource that we can no longer simply take for granted."[5.3] The Environment Agency website agreed, saying that, "in some cases existing (water abstraction) licenses are already damaging the environment."[5.4] This situation is occurring with alarming regularity and with the changing weather patterns attributable to climate change are very likely to increase.

Leaks in large scale infrastructure

The centralised water distribution network in the UK is prone to leaks and problems. The estimated rate of water loss varies considerably between companies and many have set targets, agreed by the regulator the Office of Water Services (Ofwat), which has the power to fine companies that miss targets. Over the last decade water companies have reduced the loss through leakage by about a quarter (Figure

43). However, on average over 3500 ML of water are still lost every day in the 300 000 km of water mains and reservoirs that supply over 23 million domestic customers.[5.5], [5.6] A million litres (ML) of water is roughly enough to fill 12 500 baths. This leakage figure is around a fifth of water distributed and a third of these losses occur between the road and people's houses: as these are the householder's responsibility it is unlikely they will be repaired in any great hurry. Although the level of water loss is of pressing concern, the problem of leaks remains unlikely to be solved in the foreseeable future because in the UK water is considered so abundant that it is cheaper to let the leaks continue than it is to repair them.[5.7] Yet it would seem that these repairs are merely tinkering around the edges, when it is arguably a fundamental change in the way that we collect water that is required. Figure 44 demonstrates the level of water loss through leakage between 1992 and 2005.[5.8]

Domestic water usage and increasing demand

The average volume of water consumed in the UK is 150 L per person per day (Lpd), which equates to 54 750 L or 54.75 m³ of water per person per year (Figure 44).[5.9] This water is used for a variety of activities and compares to 200 to 300 Lpd in the rest of Europe, 575 Lpd in the USA and less than 10 Lpd in Mozambique. The minimum as stipulated for survival by the United Nations Children's Fund and the World Health Organization for drinking

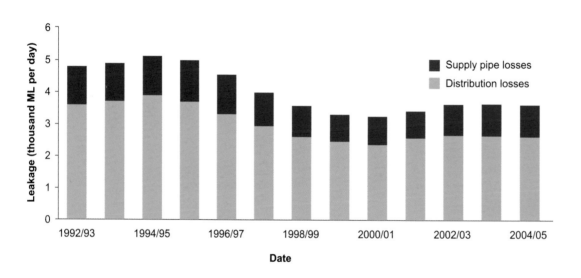

Figure 43: Daily water loss through pipe leakage. Source: Ofwat

and personal hygiene is 20 Lpd.[5.10] Other than the volume of the UK figure the other most striking aspect of this is the quality of water consumed. The water used for all activities in most houses is potable water, which includes many non-potable or non-drinking quality activities such as toilet flushing or watering the lawn. Looking at the breakdown of average use from Figure 44, 96% or 144 L of potable water are used for activities that do not need it to be refined to such a high standard and this juxtaposes starkly with the significantly increasing sale of bottled water.

Although it would seem that the level of rainfall in the UK is plentiful, there is already water stress without considering the massive plans for developing vast swathes of affordable housing over the next few decades. In the south east of England alone, under the South East Spatial Strategy, there are plans to build between 28 900 and 40 000 new homes every year for 20 years. This extra half a million or so houses can only exasperate the competition for water between people and the environment, as scarcity in summer is already an acute problem. A statistical release by the Office Deputy Prime Minister confirmed that in 2003 there were 20.9 million households in England, which will grow to 25.7 million by 2026 when various social trends, such as an ageing population, have been incorporated. This is a staggering expansion of 209 000 extra households every year for 20 years.[5.11] With such burgeoning demand, billions of pounds of water infrastructure will need to be invested in and alternative water sources, such as rainwater harvesting and greywater recycling, will need to be included to alleviate environmental degradation. This could simply happen by enjoying the rainwater that falls on our roofs.

TAPPING ALTERNATIVE WATER RESOURCES

Rainwater harvesting

People have been harvesting rainwater for millennia and there are many early examples of this technology being used by the Romans and others. In more recent times the idea has been mostly overlooked as large scale centralised collection and distribution of water is safer and more convenient.

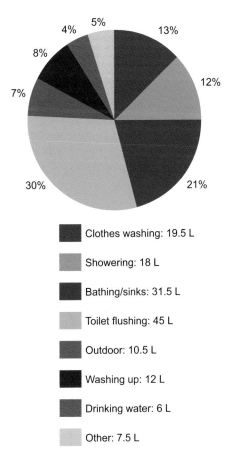

Figure 44: Average domestic daily water consumption and use. Source: Waterwise

With the increasing cost of water supply, rainwater harvesting is beginning to pay for itself with shorter payback periods: the larger the roof the faster the payback. The potential for rainwater harvesting in the UK is massive because of high levels of rainfall, and this technology is already widely deployed throughout the rest of Northern Europe.

The environmental consultancy ech2o calculates that it is possible to collect 1700 L of rain off a roof of 100 m² for every 25 mm of rainfall per year. For a typical area that receives 640 mm of rain a year, for example in the south east of England or the Midlands, 120 L a day on average can be collected and in other wetter areas such as north west England, the same roof would harvest over 200 L a day.[5.12] Meanwhile the spokesperson for the UK Rain Harvesting Association, Terry Nash, stated that in the UK last year there were 1141 rainwater harvesting installations by the associations' members, while there were probably 300 to 400 more installations outside of this figure by others.[5.13] This brings estimated figure of installed rainwater harvesting systems in UK to 15 000: in Germany over the last 15 to 20 years the figure is over 600 000 installations.

Due to the nature of the technology – the need for large underground storage tanks – such systems are difficult to fit retrospectively to existing properties in towns and cities, although one popular exception to this is rainwater collection butts, which became very popular during the drought of 2005/6 for gardeners.

However, the situation is vastly different for any new build as the tanks can easily be installed during the groundwork phase. Most systems are designed to supply rainwater to flush toilets and other non-potable activities such as clothes washing; however, with a couple of additional filters they can easily supply drinking water as well. These systems are dual supply as they are backed up with mains water, for times when the rainwater tanks are empty.

The fundamental issue with a lack of water in certain parts of the UK should not be about rainfall with the average rainfall per year between 1971 and 2000 being 1125 mm.[5.14] In some places the average would be much lower, but this highlights even more the crucial need to harvest every drop of water that falls on our roofs. From these figures it would appear that the crux of the matter is the water supply management of the country. The fact is that most buildings do not store rainwater, even though it is falling freely onto their roofs. Buildings do not have the capacity to take advantage of the precious rainwater that flows down their gutters into the drains and finally to the beleaguered sewers.

Current grey and blackwater recycling

In their homes most people use water with little thought as to where it comes from and the processes used to supply it. Water is conveniently dispatched through taps and toilet cisterns, used and then disappears down the drain to be dealt with elsewhere. All this wastewater is also mixed together so that what is often relatively innocuous wastewater, or greywater, from activities such as dishwashing, joins up with raw sewage (blackwater) and the two of them are both sent to the sewage treatment plant. That wastewater is then treated and, most often, pumped out to sea. In a situation where there are water shortages in the UK this seems to many people to be an incredibly wasteful form

of water management. This point of view has found expression in a number of initiatives to separate greywater from blackwater before the two mix together, in order to treat, recycle and reuse it for non-drinkable purposes.

Earthship pioneer, Mike Reynolds, points out the apparent fundamental craziness of this equation in his book *Water from the sky*:[5.15]

"…normally a person would use brand new fresh water from an aquifer to take a bath in. They throw that away down the drain into a sewage system and mix it with everybody else's shit and turn it into sewage. They then would use brand new fresh water again to water indoor plants. They would then use brand new fresh clean water to flush their toilet. Then they would use brand new fresh clean water again to water outside."

Instead of this, Mike Reynolds proposes 'using the same water four times to do these four tasks' through recycling the greywater in botanical (plant containing) cells, pumping the treated water to the toilet cistern for reuse, then sending sewage out to contained outdoor botanical cells.

Water recycling is a statement of how important water is as a resource, and it is also an implicit attack on the way in which water is presently treated in our society. The fact that there are so few greywater recycling schemes presently in operation in the UK illustrates how little is being done to conserve what is one of the most primary needs for human life on this planet. One of the major problems with greywater recycling is that there are no recognised standards and guidelines for the use of non-potable water; whereas potable water is highly regulated. Also, the costs associated with it are off-putting to new build developers and retrofitting homeowners alike.

Sewage (blackwater) is not quite as easy to deal with as greywater in that it is potentially much more harmful. The key environmental aim with sewage is to try and limit the impact that it has on the eco-systems that exist in and around human habitation. A reedbed solution, such as that employed at Hockerton, is an increasingly popular option for processing sewage onsite (Figure 45). The roots of reed mace (bulrush) and common reed supply oxygen to bacteria in the water which attack the pathogens that are present in the sewage.

However, for all the novel solutions to blackwater treatment the most efficient method of dealing with this type of waste is to not create it all by using compost toilets. This is illustrated by the remarkable

Figure 45: Hockerton Housing Project blackwater treatment lake

fact that sewage is actually 99.9% water and the sewage treatment process is designed to treat the 0.1% of solids contained within the water.

EARTHSHIP WATER SYSTEMS

Outline

The earthship has no connection to mains water and relies purely on rain and snow melt for its supply. The earthship water systems combine rainwater harvesting, greywater and blackwater treatment systems and other water conservation measures and have evolved through 35 years of practical experience, design and construction of many systems. The strategy is that the earthship can provide enough water to survive in any region in the world where precipitation is over 200 mm, which other than desert, forms the majority of the world. The concept is that water is harvested, filtered and then used and 're-used' four times within the earthship water system. First rainwater is captured and then purified to a level safe to drink or wash with. Secondly the wastewater that flows from all the sinks and showers (greywater) is used to water the plants in greywater planters which clean the water. The third use is for the toilet flush and lastly as blackwater or sewage, the wastewater feeds reeds and plants to be treated back to harmless water. While the water here is not literally used four times, the point is a system that extensively reuses a nutrient rich resource. In the desert and other dry regions these water systems facilitate survival, but in temperate climates such as the UK, they create a low impact model for best water conservation and onsite treatment practice. In the arid climes of Taos, New Mexico, occasionally water needs to be 'tankered' in to refill empty rainwater tanks in very dry times. This is especially true in the earthships that are rented out, as the visitors that stay in them tend to have more water intensive lifestyles and are not used to living in the desert. Table 9 summarises the different stages of the earthship water systems from the first drip to the last drop.

Collection and roof materials

Rainwater lands on the earthship roof, runs through the guttering and is then filtered before storage. From its evolution in the deserts of New Mexico, the earthship roof has been designed with a very low pitch that is orientated towards the sun in order that snow fall on the roof can melt and flow into the tanks before it evaporates. In the UK this aspect of the earthship concept will adapt to the more temperate climate as most water harvested is rain, not snow melt, and the rate of evaporation off flat roofs is much higher than that off pitched roofs. As some of the rainwater harvested will eventually be used for potable activities the choice of roof materials is crucial. The materials must be both durable and inert, to remove the possibility of chemical leachate into the drinking water supply. The decision of which roof materials to use can be much wider for rainwater systems designed only for non-potable uses. Earthship Brighton uses a combination of pro-panel steel profile metal roof and thermoplastic polyolefin (TPO) single ply membrane. The roof shape channels the rain into wide timber TPO lined guttering and where the gutter narrows the metal roof has a splash guard. At the time of construction in summer 2003, the Flagon TPO ethylene propylene/PR membrane was the only single ply membrane on the market in the UK that had Water Regulation Advisory Scheme certification. The baked enamel final finish on the surface of the pro-panel steel profile roof reduces any leachate into the water. On Earthship Fife the roof material used was ethylene propylene diene monomer (EPDM) rubber membrane. This is a material that is widely used on earthships in New Mexico and can also be used for lining the greywater planters as well, though it is higher maintenance than other roofing solutions.

Pre-filtering

At Earthship Brighton the first pre-filter is a bed of gravel built into the roof structure which removes leaves, twigs, sediment and other debris; the water then flows through a WISY vortex underground filter to remove finer particulates before the water is stored in underground eco-vat tanks. The filter uses the impetus of the flowing rainwater to create a vortex which pushes the water to the outside of the chamber through a fine mesh filter. Around 90% of the water flows through the filter and the pipe to the storage tanks, with the rest, which is mixed with detritus, falling through the centre to a wastewater runoff and soakaway. This filter requires regular cleaning every couple of months as dirt makes them less efficient and so more water is lost to drainage. There is also a plan to put an extra tank on this overflow pipe to collect the water for irrigating the surrounding organic farm.

Rainfall yield and storage

In Earthship Brighton the size of the storage tanks are much larger than most domestic rainwater harvesting systems. Most rainwater systems are only designed to store 4000 to 5000 L and a mains water backup, if needed, can charge the tank for when the volume of the tank drops below 5%.

Table 10 illustrates the annual rainfall yields for Earthship Brighton and Earthship Fife using the equation of annual rainfall yield = roof area × average annual rainfall × runoff coefficient × filter efficiency.[5.16]

Annually, Earthship Brighton can harvest up to 47 970 L or 47.97 m³ of water and since rainwater harvesting began in August 2003 the tanks have always been at least half full, even though tens of thousands of litres of water have been used for local agricultural irrigation. Although the tanks have a large capacity they do overflow several times a year

Water type	No	Stage
Rainwater	1	Collection
	2	Pre-filtering
	3	Storage
	4	Potable and non-potable filtering
	5	First use for drinking, sinks and shower
Greywater	6	Removal of grease and other particles
	7	Second use – indoor treatment by plants
	8	Pump 'recycled water' to toilet cistern
	9	Third use – toilet flush
Blackwater	10	Blackwater settles in septic tank
	11	Fourth use – outdoor treatment by plants
	12	Clean water soakaway

Table 9: Stages of the earthship water systems

after heavy rainstorms, which is important to lose the particles that float on top of the water. Using this figure, the water systems, assuming the average daily consumption of 150 L, would provide 320 days of water or 80 days for a family of four. In practice the actual consumption figure would be considerably lower as there are other technologies in place in the earthship to reduce the demand. For example, one of the features of the earthship water system is that different types of nutrient rich wastewater are treated separately with plants at each stage, maximising reuse at every opportunity and minimising the amount of water needed. If the system was designed to the normal capacity of 18 days storage then the cistern size could be downsized to around 4600 L.

In Earthship Brighton there are four eco-vat tanks; each has a volume of 5000 L, and they are linked in series to create a total storage capacity of 20 000 L (Table 11). This, coupled with other water conservation measures, is enough for two to three month's supply based on average annual rainfall patterns for the Sussex area. The tanks are buried

into the hill and below the roof level, but above the level to supply the earthship, so the whole system is gravity fed until it reaches the filtration panel inside the building. Underground tanks also offer a dark, cool environment that tends to discourage bacterial growth. There is a rainfall tank gauge inside the earthship to allow easy reading of the amount of water stored.

Potable and non-potable filtering

The rainwater is drawn down by gravity from the underground water tanks to the water organising module to be treated to two standards: non-potable and potable (Table 12). The two stage filtration process reflects the fact that most of the water used

Figure 48: Rain storage tanks before burial (Earthship Brighton)

Figure 46: Diagram of Earthship Brighton roof harvesting rain

Figure 47: Roof materials (Earthship Brighton)

Figure 49: Rain storage tanks after burial, and roof (Earthship Brighton)

Table 10: Annual rainfall yields for Earthship Brighton and Earthship Fife

	Roof area	Average annual rainfall	Run-off or drainage coefficient	Filter efficiency	Annual yield
Unit	(m²)	(mm)	–	–	(m³/year)
Earthship Brighton	135.00	789.70	0.5	0.9	47.97
Earthship Fife	31.50	676.20	0.5	0.9	9.60

Table 11: Earthship Brighton and Fife rain harvesting systems summary

	Earthship Brighton	Earthship Fife
Average annual rainfall	789.7 mm*	676.2 mm**
Average number of days with more than 1 mm rain	115*	121**
Roof area	135 m²	31.5 m²
Roof material/surface	Thermoplastic polyolefin single ply membrane/stainless steel profile	EPDM rubber membrane
Roof pitch	4°C	Flat
Average rainfall yield	47.97 m³ or 47 970 L	9.60 m³ or 9.60 L
Pre-tank filters	Gravel/0.28 mm WISY vortex	Gravel
Storage tanks	Eco-vat tanks	Re-used water tank
Storage capacity	20 m³ or 20 000 L	4.546 m³ or 4546 L

* Meteorological Office figure using the Eastbourne weather station average between 1971 and 2000.

** Meteorological Office figure using the Edinburgh weather station average between 1971 and 2000.

Table 12: Water organising module components (see Figure 50)

Module number	Output/component	Purpose
Non-potable water		
1	60 μ mesh filter	Protects pump from sediment
2	12 V DC pump	Pressurises system to 3.45 bar
3	500 μ mesh filter	Removes finer particulates
4	Water meter	Measures volume of non-potable water treated for regular filter cleaning
Potable water		
5	Charcoal filter	Protects drinking water filter
6	Doulton ultracarb carbon block filter	Removes pathogens, trace organics and inorganics such as chlorine and lead
7	Watersource S/S Ultra Violet System	Renders bacteria harmless
8	Water meter	Measures volume of potable water treated for regular filter cartridge change or cleaning

in domestic and commercial buildings does not need to be purified to a drinking water standard. The water is first passed through a 60 μ mesh filter to remove sediment and this filter serves to protect the 12 V DC pump, which with the aid of a pressure tank pressurises the system to 3.45 bar or conventional household pressure. The pump is adequate to push the water through the 500 μ mesh filter into the pressure tank. After the pump there is a finer grade mesh filter and now the water is ready for most uses including showering, bathing, washing clothes and cleaning dishes. All of these filters are removable and can be easily cleaned: this is the main house supply.

To treat the water to a drinking water standard the water is filtered using charcoal, carbon block and ultraviolet light filters. Under the 1999 Clean Water Supply Act because of the potential contamination from bird faeces, rainwater is classified as raw sewage so thorough filtration for the removal of pathogens and other harmful elements is critical for a safe wholesome supply. After the water organising module, the water system is a typical domestic system (Figure 50). In both Earthship Brighton and Earthship Fife the basic water organising module was purchased as pre-constructed units from Earthship Biotecture and shipped from the USA, with the extra drinking water filters being sourced in the UK.

Low intensity chemical free greywater recycling

In earthships the first use of water is in the sinks and shower, and all sinks have a hot, cold and drinking water tap. The wastewater, or greywater, that is generated flows through a grease and particle filter into an EPDM rubber-lined greywater planter or botanical treatment cell. This lining creates a closed area that becomes its own eco-system that adapts to the treatment of wastewater. There are various designs for grease and particle filters, but the simplest is a nylon stocking clamped over the end of the pipe, which needs to be changed once a month of so depending on use. A stainless steel clamp is used for all fittings in the planters.

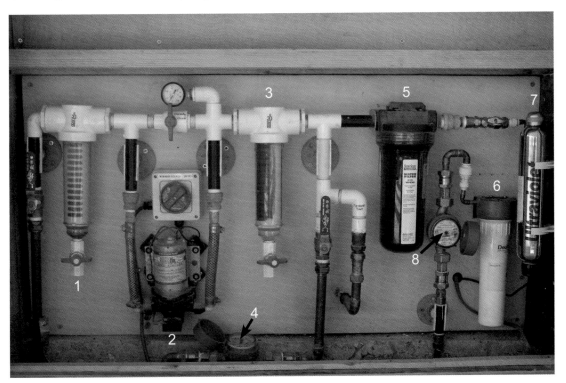

Figure 50: Water organising module (Earthship Brighton) (see Table 12 for reference to numbers)

The filter is inside a box with a hole drilled in the bottom of it and is then a placed over a pile of 75 mm rocks or rock 'bulbs', which enable showers and other large volumes of water to percolate into the system very quickly (Figures 51 and 52). These bulbs are also placed at all plumbing junctions to facilitate fast draining between sections through increased areas or voids between the rocks.

The greywater planters are designed to recycle greywater through a variety of natural processes, such as transpiration, evaporation, oxygenation and through the rhizosphere or treatment by the bacteria that live around plant's root systems.[5.17] These processes deal with the various constituent parts of greywater, by consuming the suspended solids and reducing the bacteria level, the grease and fat having already been removed by an earlier filter. It is recommended that 2.33 m² of planter are needed for each plumbing fixture.[5.15] Earthship Brighton has a kitchen sink, bathroom sink and a shower; this means that the minimum planter area of 7 m² would be required. The two greywater planters, located in the conservatory and meeting room and linked in series have a combined area of 12.75 m², which means that 10% of the useable floor space is lost to greywater treatment. It is possible to link up as many greywater planters as required to treat the greywater, however, the only stipulation is that the greywater level must be the same throughout (Table 13).

The planter is made up of layers of up to 450 mm of 20 mm pea shingle, 75 mm sand and 150 mm of topsoil (Figures 53 to 55). This structure is a growing medium and stabilising environment for the plants and maximises the opportunity for them to 'encounter' the greywater. The level of the greywater comes up to the height of the pea shingle, effectively forming a greywater table with the sand keeping the soil from clogging up the gravel. The greywater planters are located next to the south facing windows, creating a very beneficial environment for the plants which thrive in the nutrient rich greywater and sunlight. In summer as the plants grow they offer increased shading from the intensity of the sun and in winter can be cut back to increase the solar gain into the earthship (Figure 56).

At this stage the water has not been mixed with human waste; all blackwater is dealt with later in the process. The greywater planters have a three-way divert valve, which can be used so that the greywater directly bypasses the planter system and is discharged to the septic tank (Figures 57 and 58). The whole earthship water system deals with the water one step at a time, which makes it easier to treat in a low intensity fashion with plants in low volumes. This approach differs greatly from the centralised municipal system which has to deal with all greywater, blackwater, chemicals, organic waste and other contaminants as a sewage 'soup'; therefore it has to be very large scale to deal with the waste en masse. The greywater system in earthships

Figure 51: Rock bulb installation during greywater construction (Earthship Brighton)

Figure 52: Plan view of greywater sump and rock bulbs during construction (Earthship Brighton)

Figure 53: Filling a greywater planter with 10 mm gravel (Earthship Brighton)

Figure 55: Raking gravel flat in a greywater planter (Earthship Brighton)

Figure 54: Sand raked flat in a greywater planter (Earthship Brighton)

Figure 56: Fully planted greywater planter (Earthship Fife)

Table 13: Comparison of greywater systems in Earthship Brighton and Earthship Fife

	Earthship Brighton	Earthship Fife
Fittings	Kitchen sink/ bathroom sink/ shower	2 sinks
Number of planters	2.00*	1.00
Length (m)	15.00	5.00
Width (m)	0.85	1.40
Minimum depth (m)	0.60	0.60
Maximum depth (m)	1.20	1.40
Area (m²)	12.75	7.00
Planter area as a percentage of total floor space	10.5%	22%
Filters	Activated charcoal	Sphagnum moss/ activated charcoal

*For the purposes of calculation the two planters are treated as one entity.

Figure 58: Septic tank installation (Earthship Brighton)

Figure 57: Greywater feed pipe for toilet and pump panel (Earthship Brighton)

is designed so that there is no human contact with the greywater and no opportunity for backwash – this is important to avoid risk of infection (Table 13).

The choices of household cleaners that can be poured down the sink in an earthship are limited to those that will avoid upsetting the balance of the plants, bacteria and greywater eco-system. In this method of water treatment the plants and the eco-system around them are the system. This is equally important with the chemicals used to clean the toilet which can impair the anaerobic bacteria that live in the septic tank and reedbed. As the system is comprised of natural components it takes a while for the plants to settle in and the whole greywater colony to evolve. In the first year the treated water may be discoloured as the plants establish themselves.

Choice of plants

There are various plants that can be planted in the greywater planter, but some of the most popular edible varieties are bananas, lemon and lime trees, grapes and avocados. The larger plants suck up and treat larger volumes of greywater than those that grow on the surface. In the dry arid desert of New Mexico the planters are used to grow food and this aspect is now being explored with the extension of the planter systems, sometimes with a second greenhouse on the front of the building to incorporate large areas for food production (the Phoenix Earthship is the most contemporary example). In the temperate growing climate of the UK this area of development is not as crucial, although it would extend the growing season throughout the year and also demonstrates the innovative onsite reuse of wastewater and the possibilities of using this vastly undervalued resource.

Blackwater recycling – using plants to treat sewage

After treatment, the greywater gathers in a well at the end of the planter, until the toilet is flushed, which draws through water to fill the toilet cistern. The toilet also has a rainwater connection to give the choice between flushing with rainwater or greywater and means that advantage can be taken of periods of heavy rainfall. There is a recirculation pipe between the two planters, powered by a dedicated solar panel and a 12 V DC pump, which keeps the greywater moving continually through the treatment process until it is needed for toilet flushing, and ensures a higher quality of greywater. The separate power supply does not use power from the main house supply, but only works when it is sunny. There is a dual feed into the Earthship Brighton toilet; either greywater or rainwater can be supplied.

The earthship has no connection to the municipal sewage system; however in the UK, due to confines of space, this may not be practical for earthship developments in towns and cities. Blackwater is defined as water that has been mixed with human waste and the autonomous sewage system contains and treats all blackwater onsite. In Earthship Brighton the blackwater is discharged to settle in a 2800 L

Klargester Alpha septic tank, located 20 m from the earthship, which then overflows to a 60 m² EPDM rubber lined reedbed and finally a soakaway. The Environment Agency granted permission for a facility to deal with wastewater in this manner in 2004 and is generally very supportive of the project.

There are many different designs for the treatment of blackwater and Earthship Fife uses an alternative system very similar in design to the greywater planters (Figure 59). The blackwater flows down a soil pipe to settle in an 'infiltrator' before overflowing into two 25 mm thick Voltex lined planters in a greenhouse and the same natural processes outlined in the section above break down the sewage and the plants feed on the waste. Voltex is a waterproofing membrane, which are two geotextile layers with sodium bentonite clay sandwiched in between. The infiltrator stores the solid waste, which slowly breaks through the continual process of it drying out and liquid waste washing over it every time the toilet is flushed. The two planters measure 3×4 m and 1 m deep and linked in series side by side. The constituents of the planters are very similar to the greywater planter outlined above and are made up of 500 mm of 20 mm pea shingle, 100 mm sand and 400 mm of topsoil. The heights of the different strata vary as the shingle is deepest next to the infiltrator and slopes away to a shallower depth at the other end.

CONCLUSION

The greenhouse is an important addition in the Scottish climate as it stops flooding of the system by rainwater, increases the temperature for the plants and provides an opportunity for blackwater treatment all year round. Although Earthship Fife is a visitor's centre the capacity of the system is designed to deal with the sewage of a family of four, approximately 0.5 t of sewage per year. In domestic situations the system would be sized on the number occupants. This sewage system has been approved by the local building control authority and Scottish Environment Protection Agency.[5.18]

The systems that have been installed in Earthship Brighton and Earthship Fife are experimental and need to be monitored closely. The purified rainwater from Earthship Brighton is in the process of being tested by the local authority's environmental health department and a system of close monitoring will

Figure 59: Blackwater treatment system (Earthship Fife)

need to be put into place before occupancy. Once the earthship is being used every day then accurate data can be gathered regarding the rainfall yield, quality and adequacy of the rain harvesting systems and the grey and blackwater recycling for end-use consumption can be accessed. It should be noted that these 'living' systems are designed for domestic purposes, and yet they have been installed in public buildings that have different needs. To compensate for this in Earthship Fife, members of staff in the building simulate a 'domestic situation' of running the tap for five minutes and flushing the toilet a few times to feed the grey and blackwater planters. As a demonstration model this is fine, but clearly not an example of best water-conservation practice, although it would of course be different if people lived in Earthship Fife. The systems may also need further tweaking to work more effectively in the UK climate. For example it is possible that the evaporation rate in the UK climate may be less than at certain times in New Mexico, so future earthship builds may need a greater surface area of planter. Consistent monitoring of the water systems over the next couple of years will allow for more thorough designs for the next generation of UK earthships.

REFERENCES AND NOTES

[5.1] See www.metoffice.gov.uk/climate/uk/location/england.

[5.2] See www.environment agency.gov.uk/regions/midlands.

[5.3] See www.defra.gov.uk/corporate/ministers/statements/em060301.htm.

[5.4] See www.environment-agency.gov.uk.

[5.5] See www.ofwat.gov.uk/aptrix/ofwat/publish.nsf/Content/navigation-ofwat-faqs-statistics.

[5.6] See www.ofwat.gov.uk/aptrix/ofwat/publish.nsf/Content/customers_in_eng_wales.

[5.7] Stauffer J (1996). Safe to drink? The quality of your water. Machynnlleth, Centre of Alternative Technology Publications.

[5.8] See www.ofwat.gov.uk.

[5.9] See www.waterwise.org.uk.

[5.10] Watkins (2006). Human Development Report 2006: Beyond scarcity: Power, poverty and the global water crisis. New York, United Nations Development Programme.

[5.11] See www.communities.gov.uk/index.asp?id=1002882&PressNoticeID=2097.

[5.12] ech2o are environmental consultants offering design advice and seminars on all aspects of sustainable water use, low or zero carbon energy systems, carbon literacy and environmental choice of materials. See www.ech2o.co.uk.

[5.13] See www.ukhra.org.

[5.14] See www.metoffice.gov.uk/climate/uk/averages/19712000/index.html.

[5.15] Reynolds M (2005). Water from the sky. Taos, New Mexico, Solar Survival Press.

[5.16] Parsloe C (2005). CIBSE knowledge series: reclaimed water. London, The Chartered Institute of Building Services Engineers (CIBSE).

[5.17] Leggett D J, Brown R, Brewer D and Holliday E (2001). Rainwater and greywater use in buildings: Decision making for water conservation. London, CIRIA.

[5.18] Cowie P (2004). The earthship toolkit: Your guide to building a zero waste zero energy future. Kinghorn, Sustainable Communities Initiatives.

Earthships show how materials such as tyres, which are usually considered to be waste, can be used as effective building materials

CHAPTER 6
BUILDING WITH WASTE

INTRODUCTION

The disposal of waste van and car tyres is a large scale problem in the UK, and one that has recently got tangibly worse due to the implementation in July 2006 of the EU Landfill Directive 1999/31/EC that completely banned the disposal of all waste tyres and their components to landfill. In 2004 alone there were, according to DTI statistics, approximately 48 million waste tyres generated in the UK. Of these, 34% were recycled, 26% reused, 15% burned as fuel, 7% exported and 6% used in landfill engineering applications. Only 12% of used tyres went to landfill while it was still legal in 2004. This on its own still represented a massive 58 797 t of material that now needs to find a use.[6.1] For earthships, used tyres are far from redundant – they form the fundamental building block to the structure while also embodying some of their key principles. And tyres are not the only type of waste used in building earthships – bottles, cans, salvaged masonry and timber all form part of the fabric of these buildings as well.

This chapter examines the reasons and efficacy of building with different waste materials, and looks in some detail at the legal and regulatory basis for building with tyres. This is of significant interest due to the pathfinding nature of the first UK earthship builds in exploring this position; as pioneers the foundations have been laid for future tyre based builds benefiting from more regulatory clarity and certainty.

Figure 60: A disused quarry – the Hampole tyre dump, near Doncaster. Copyright Chemical Hazards and Poisons Division (London), Health Protection Agency

Figure 61: Rammed tyre wall (Earthship Fife)

Figure 62: Rammed tyre walls (Earthship Brighton)

WHY USE TYRES?

One of the initial drivers in using tyres as a building block in earthship design was simply to find a use for some of the millions of tyres being thrown away globally every day. Rather than using materials that require manufacture specifically for the purpose of the building – such as bricks, for example – the earthship, as much as possible, attempts to reuse abundant materials that otherwise would be recycled (potentially, as in this case, from non-construction related activities) and require low levels of energy to bring onto site and use in the building. Reusing materials is always a more efficient use of resources than recycling as it uses less energy. The tyre, which Mike Reynolds describes as being "indigenous all over the world as a 'natural resource'",[6.2] is ideal under these criteria, not least because it has such a generic design (no specialist sourcing required) and can be used for the purposes of building without any chemical or mechanical modification. "The very quality of tyres that makes them a problem to society (the fact they won't go away) makes them an ideal durable building material for earthships".[6.3]

The Waste and Resources Action Programme (WRAP) has said that "As most used tyres can no longer be sent to landfill, they have to be used in some form or other, therefore they are a valuable resource. Current uses include export, reuse, retreading, shredding/crumbing, used as a fuel, landfill engineering as shred or bales." The organisation also said that "… earthships as a great use of used tyres and we are aware of a number of UK examples". The WRAP tyres programme was started in April 2005 to "break down the barriers to the collection, segregation and reprocessing of waste tyres, to develop alternative end uses for the recovered material, and to develop their markets".[6.4] The Environment Agency, significantly, has also recognised the need for alternatives to waste tyre disposal. For the innovative work the project was undertaking by reusing and recycling tyres and other materials, Earthship Brighton received support from the waste company Biffa in the form of a grant via the Landfill Tax Credit Scheme (LTCS). The LTCS has a variety of objects from the remediation of land, nature conservation, and increasing biodiversity to sustainable waste management. The Low Carbon Trust was supported under the latter object of sustainable waste management: projects that encourage the development of products from waste or markets for recycled products through research, education or information dissemination. The grant of £180 000 was the lion's share of money raised for the Earthship Brighton project, but is unavailable for future sustainable waste management projects as this category was removed on 1 April 2003.[6.5]

WRAP and the Environment Agency are not the only organisations to endorse the approach to waste tyres exemplified by earthships. The government's chief scientist and chairman of the Royal Society, Sir David King, has emphasised the need for the development of what he describes as 'smart' buildings, which can consume their own rubbish and power themselves, with an emphasis on dwellings reducing their overall impact on the environment.[6.6] The earthship is a building that 'swallows waste' by actually using it as an integral part of its structure.

Sir David King's remarks also echo the sentiments of a 2006 report by the Institute for Public Policy Research (IPPR), calling for the UK to become a 'zero waste' country, where rubbish is recycled or reused – for example in energy production – instead of being sent directly to landfill. The report also

Figure 63: Exposed wall section (Earthship Brighton)

argues strongly in favour of taxation to be applied to disposable goods, encouraging people to conserve resources and buy products that will last longer. "We have become an increasingly throwaway society, reliant on cheap, disposable and hard to recycle goods," said IPPR's director, Nick Pearce.[6.6]

All this suggests that recycling as a fundamental principle at the heart of society is gaining momentum in the UK. However, the current rate of recycling glass in the UK of 35%, for example, compares unfavourably with mainland European countries where recycling of 80 to 90% has been achieved.[6.7] And yet, as Nick Pearce points out, there is a strong counter momentum in terms of the abundance of disposable, throwaway goods and products with short lifespans and little or no possibility of recycling. So the message is certainly mixed and the underlying fact underpinning all of it is that in developed countries such as the UK there is a resource requirement which needs three planets to support it. The earthship, by contrast, is a building concept that is supportive of the idea of sustainable resource use based on a 'one planet eco footprint'. So the essential materials philosophy is to try and use, wherever possible, what has been discarded and is considered redundant by the rest of society, including materials such as tyres. But it is not the tyres in themselves that are of key importance – what is important is the concept of using waste as an integral part of constructing highly effective and efficient buildings. This is why many other forms of waste, or salvaged materials, are also being used in earthships, including glass bottles, old masonry, timber, aluminium cans and plastics. And by making something incredibly useful out of 'junk', there is a genuine provocation to a wasteful society in terms of asking what other purposes 'rubbish' could be used for.

Recycling, though, is not the only advantage of using tyres as a material. They also allow another vital material to become easily manageable, a material that by its very name indicates that it is absolutely core to these structures: earth. One of the most important factors about earth is that it does not have to be transported onto site using fossil fuel, it is already there. And unlike traditional rammed earth buildings, rammed tyres do not need to be so fussy about the type of earth that is used despite there being some slight generic similarities in methodology. This is because instead of ramming earth into formwork section by section in order to construct walls (rammed earth buildings), earthships are constructed by ramming earth into tyres with sledgehammers. The tyres are then stacked on top of one another in order to construct the walls of the earthship. Ramming tyres is an essentially low

skill technique that is easy to learn and transfer whereas rammed earth construction is a highly skilled and precise technique that requires genuine expertise. The correct soil composition is essential to the viability of a rammed earth wall as the wall is freestanding and liable to structural weakness if the wrong type of earth is used. By ramming earth into tyres, though, individual building blocks with absolute structural integrity and great mass are created. The technique is also extremely simple and requires a minimal amount of training for new practitioners to learn.

Tyre ramming, or 'pounding tyres', as it is popularly known by exponents of earthship construction, is an extremely low tech process that simply requires earth, a conventional car or van tyre, a piece of cardboard to prevent the earth from falling through the tyre, a sledgehammer and someone who is unafraid of a few blisters. The earth is packed in by hand to begin with then compacted with the sledgehammer until it is firm. The process continues, ramming as much as 75 kg of earth into the tyre, until it is packed tightly and swollen by about 25% from its original depth. The tyre then needs to be levelled to ensure that it can form a stable building block. The stability also comes from this building

Figure 64: Tyre pounding in action (Taos, New Mexico)

block being so wide: at just under 1 m in thickness, earthship tyre walls are three to four times thicker than conventional walls meaning that they do not require conventional foundations.

Due to the low tech approach and reuse of waste without modification the carbon emissions from producing this 'brick' are negligible, although time consuming. And the resultant product has some notable qualities: in particular it is highly durable and is a great thermal mass building material. Indeed, Mike Reynolds has said: "If I was paid $30 million to invent the best thermal mass brick I could, I would invent a tyre."[6.8] Thermal mass is absolutely crucial to the design of earthships; coupled with the passive solar capacity of the building, thermal mass enables the structure to soak up large amounts of energy from the sun. This energy is retained by the walls and 'radiated' back into the building at night. The energy saved from space heating is enormous, with space heating forming approximately 60% of the average UK household's energy use.[6.9] This requirement is almost entirely avoided in the earthship due to its thermal mass and passive solar capacity.

Tyres, therefore, are an excellent material for earthships in helping to fulfil a number of primary aims of the structure: to build with recycled materials and use as little embodied energy as possible, to integrate large amounts of thermal mass into the structure to virtually eliminate space heating requirements and to provide a stable and durable low maintenance structure to shelter the inhabitants from the elements. As noted by Sutherland Lyall in the *Architects' Journal*, there is probably a marked degree of scepticism in the architectural community in general about the use of tyres as a structural device. "Architects", he wrote, "may cavil at a used tyre main structural element, especially when the tyres just sit on the local Brighton chalk, scraped back to an undisturbed layer." [6.10] Indeed, some architects feel that tyres are simply not an appropriate material in any sense for a serious building. But the earthship is a refutation of that sentiment and he goes on to assuage the doubts of the anti-tyre brigade. "…we are too used to complicated and responsibility proofed modern foundation systems" he argues. "It turns out that earth/chalk filled used tyres spread relatively light domestic loads very efficiently – a proposition which building control was not disposed to fault. As the steep, internal side of the berm, they worked successfully as a retaining wall."[6.10]

Figure 65: Section of Earthship Brighton showing rammed tyre wall at rear and footing at front

LEGISLATIVE AND REGULATORY POSITION FOR BUILDING WITH TYRES

Building with what is classified as waste, though, has not been an entirely straightforward process from a legal point of view, due in the main to the Waste Management Licensing Regulations (1994) which require, among other things, that all activities involving waste are either licenced or exempted. This provides a framework to 'track' waste and ensure that it is being disposed of responsibly and under controlled conditions. The EU Landfill Directive 1999/31/EC has an impact in the sense that it makes it imperative that other uses are found for waste tyres. This is because the EU legislation completely banned the dumping of all conventional tyres in landfill from July 2006, whereas previously it had remained legal to dump shredded tyres in landfill after an initial ban on dumping whole tyres in 2003. The positive aspect of this legislation is that it ensures that tyres are not just discarded after they have served their primary use. Instead, as the Environment Agency and WRAP have both said, alternative uses need to be found for these tyres. However, the negative aspect of the present legislative framework is that it has complicated permissions for building earthships in the UK.

Earthship Fife was the first earthship to apply for an exemption to the waste licensing regulations (1994) under schedule 3, paragraph 15, on the grounds of 'beneficial use of waste'. It is under this exemption, for example, that tyres can be used as fenders on boats and as a swing in a children's playground. The other type of exemption is a paragraph 19 exemption that covers certain, specific and named types of waste to be used for construction purposes, an example of which includes certain types of demolition waste being reused as hardcore. However, a paragraph 19 exemption does not specifically name used tyres – either whole, shredded, crumbed or baled – so this exemption cannot apply.

An application from Earthship Fife was made to the Scottish Environmental Protection Agency (SEPA) and the exemption was duly granted (exemption reference number WMX/E/0003204). However, when Earthship Brighton made a similar application on the same grounds to the Environment Agency in

England in autumn 2002 it was rejected. This may seem surprising, particularly considering the fact that although Scottish Law is different to English Law, the waste management licensing regulations are exactly the same in both countries. But there are in fact a couple of reasons why the inconsistency occurred on this occasion. The first reason is that the definition of waste had changed since the time of SEPA's exemption and that of the application for an exemption in Brighton. The change in the definition of waste incorporated more items as 'waste' than previously; and not only did the category widen but the items classified as being waste remained 'waste' for a longer period of time. This made the regulators think harder about waste and re-evaluating all associated issues. The paragraph 15 exemption (beneficial use of waste) that Earthship Brighton had applied for is pertinent only if the waste being used is not processed or changed in any way from its original form. Although the rubber in a tyre is not changed by ramming with earth, the tyre itself becomes solid and its physical form is changed. The Environment Agency therefore deemed that a paragraph 15 exemption did not apply in this case. The second conceivable reason for the inconsistency between SEPA's ruling and that of the Environment Agency's is the possibility that SEPA's position was not strictly in accordance with legal precedent. Looking at some case law suggests that the Environment Agency's decision that a paragraph 15 exemption would not apply in the case of Earthship Brighton is a decision that would have been upheld in court.

The fact that an exemption was not granted, though, was not the end of the story. Realising the groundbreaking nature and unusual circumstances of the Brighton build, the Environment Agency decided to take an extraordinary position by allowing the project to continue without an exemption or a licence. For the sake of clarity it is worth quoting extensively from the letter sent by the Environment Agency to the directors of the company building the earthship – the Low Carbon Network Ltd (LCN) – in February 2003:

"As the legislation stands at the present time there is no exemption from the need to hold a waste management (licence) for the activity you wish to carry out. As such a waste management licence would be needed if you wish to continue with the project. However I am in sympathy with the trials you wish to carry out, and your desire to

Figure 66: Interior view of glass bottle brick bathroom wall at the Jacobsen earthship (Taos, New Mexico)

demonstrate and prove the concept, particularly with respect to Building Regulations issues. I have also noted that this is the first project of its type in the UK. Accordingly therefore I have taken the exceptional step of giving you authority to carry on with the demonstration project without the need for a waste management licence. This letter can be taken as that authority. I must make it clear that, as a demonstration trial for the UK, this has to be a one-off situation and that it forms no precedent for any further requests from you, or other groups across the country."

Most importantly at the time, this gave the go-ahead for Earthship Brighton to proceed with construction. This go-ahead took the form of an 'enforcement position' which was a local decision, made by the regulators (the Environment Agency) on the basis that the earthship was a 'low risk' activity and that a waste management licence was not appropriate. This recognised the fact that technically LCN were acting unlawfully but the regulatory powers would not be enforced in this case. This only applied to Earthship Brighton. At the time this did not set a precedent and individual enforcement positions were still necessary for other builds.

But a subsequent invitation from the Environment Agency for LCN to participate in a stakeholder dialogue, created the opportunity for significant lobbying to ensure that future earthship builds would not have to labour under the same regulatory and legislative ambiguities. The result of this dialogue was a report issued in June 2004 on seeking solutions for waste tyres entitled *Required exemptions to waste management licensing for tyre recovery*.[6.11] The needs of earthship builders were taken into account in this report which was recommended to Department for Environment, Food and Rural Affairs (DEFRA) by the Environment Agency. Among the recommendations was a key amendment to paragraph 19 of the 1994 legislation to allow whole tyres as a waste form used in construction. Until these recommendations are enshrined in law, the Environment Agency has stated that it will take the 'lightest regulatory stance' to future earthship builds, providing that the local authority has granted planning permission.

The Environment Agency recognises the 'low risk' posed by earthship construction, as seen in the examination of the specific environmental risks posed by building with tyres. Due to a new risk assessment system at the Environment Agency this makes evaluation of whether to allow builds to go ahead a much easier decision to take than previously. Now low risk waste activities are brought to a national panel every six weeks by local environment officers who assess the risk and make a decision whether to allow the activity to take place. The system is specifically designed for activities such as earthship construction. It is not an exemption or a waste management licence but it is a pragmatic position that allows for earthships to be built now with relatively little bureaucracy until such time as the amendment is made to the 1994 legislation. It has been anecdotally reported to the authors of this book that in 2006 there was a photograph of an earthship tyre wall on the Environment Agency internal intranet system as a specific example of a 'low risk activity'. Whether or not this is true in a sense is immaterial; all the evidence points to the fact that under the low risk classification, the Environment Agency is demonstrating a supportive regulatory position towards future earthship construction.

Figure 67: Aluminium can wall (Earthship Fife)

Figure 68: Volunteer cutting glass bottles with a wet tile cutter (Earthship Brighton)

The fire risk, despite what might intuitively be thought, is also practically non-existent. This was demonstrated when an earthship in the USA was burnt in a forest fire. The only parts left of the earthship were the tyre and glass bottle walls. In fact, trying to burn a tyre rammed with earth is exceptionally difficult and consequently forms a negligible risk.

Rammed tyres are an essentially inert building block that in earthships are protected from the elements by a thermal wrap (50 to 100 mm barrier of rigid insulation) and a damp proof membrane around the outside. Stability and wrapping means that they do not emit chemicals in the form of leachates or gases. These environmental risk assessments have been accepted by both the Environment Agency and SEPA and demonstrate that the environmental and structural risks of building with tyres are extremely low. And there is practically no fire risk involved. This point needs to be repeated because of the common perception that a building made from tyres must be highly flammable. This is certainly not true in the case of earthships.

SPECIFIC RISK ASSESSMENT CONCERNS WITH TYRES

In terms of the environmental risk assessment for tyres, the specific original concerns about their use were centred on the issues of durability, fire risk, leachates and off-gassing. These concerns were valid and appropriate due to the groundbreaking nature of using tyres as a building material and it gave earthship builders the opportunity to gain more credibility through the technique undergoing considerable scrutiny. In terms of durability there are very few concerns about tyres as they are relatively inert and do not degrade except by exposure to sunlight and erosion by water. However, for Earthship Fife, Scottish Building Control provided a five year licence for the building on the basis that the longevity of tyres was an essentially untested element. Anecdotal evidence points to the fact that tyres are actually highly stable and durable as building blocks, with the oldest earthships in New Mexico having been around for 25 years to date. Moreover, the tyres themselves are protected from the elements in the structure of the building by plastering within the structure and the damp proofing on the outside.

OTHER RULES ABOUT WASTE HANDLING

Nonetheless, because of the classification of tyres as waste there remain strict rules about their storage and transport. For example, the 1994 waste management legislation states that a maximum of 1000 tyres only are to be kept in secure storage onsite at any time for a maximum of one month. It also states that the waste tyres must be transported by a registered waste carrier (it is possible for an individual to register as one for about £120). The 'duty of care' of whoever is transporting and storing the tyres requires that a copy of the transfer note for each delivery of waste tyres be kept.

CONCLUSION: THE CURRENT REGULATORY POSITION FOR TYRES

In essence the regulatory position is that there are no restrictions on building earthships unless the project is considered not to be 'low risk'. However, the precedents to date are single structure projects only,

Figure 69: Glass bottle brick wall (Earthship Brighton)

Figure 70: Glass bottle brick wall showing 'porcupining' (Earthship Brighton)

Figure 71: Close up of a glass bottle brick wall during construction (Earthship Brighton)

Figure 72: Finished glass bottle brick wall with render (Earthship Brighton)

so multiple earthships are still an unknown quantity from this perspective. As long as the waste is handled responsibly and issues of transport and storage of waste tyres on site are addressed in accordance with the rules, there should not be any problems with individual earthship builds. Earthships will be allowed on this basis, subject to certain conditions that would be assessed on a site-by-site basis, as with any other development. The first step to gaining approval is to get planning permission and then ask the local Environment Agency environment officer to put the proposal forward to the low risk waste panel. Both Earthship Brighton and Earthship Fife have been instrumental in arriving at this regulatory position and they should be recognised as pioneers in finding the way for building with tyres in the UK.

OTHER LOW EMBODIED ENERGY MATERIALS

As pointed out in the introduction to this chapter, tyres may be the 'headline material' of earthships but they are far from being the only form of waste that is being used in their construction. The general materials concept is to try and reuse as many waste materials as possible. Instead of packing out the spaces between tyres solely with cement, infilling with various waste is used to try and reduce the amount of cement being used overall. Non-loadbearing walls in particular offer the opportunity to experiment with different types of 'brick' that might otherwise merely be discarded into landfill. These include aluminium cans and glass bottles. Mike Reynolds states that "the material we have found … is a little durable aluminium brick that appears 'naturally' on this planet. It is indigenous to most parts of the planet that are heavily populated. It is also known as the aluminium beverage can".[6.12] The aluminium can is often used in US earthships to create eye catching features such as panel walls, domes and vaults. This technique evolved in the desert in the 1970s where there was no recycling infrastructure. The visual effect when the technique is employed well is, perhaps surprisingly, striking and modern and it is a further reminder of what can be achieved with a waste product. However, non-ferrous metals have the highest embodied energy of any material that is used in volume in any industry or sector in society and it is better that they are

Figure 73: Exterior view of glass bottle brick bathroom wall at the Jacobsen earthship (Taos, New Mexico)

conventionally recycled in order to save the need for virgin aluminium and the further extraction of bauxite, the raw mineral for aluminium.

Glass bottle walls also form a visually impressive feature in many earthships. They can be shaped remarkably easily into 'bricks' by cutting the necks from two bottles with a generic cutting tool and sticking them together with some tape. The result is a uniform cylinder that is easy to work with, in creating a non-loadbearing wall. This significantly reduces the embodied energy that would come in the form of a brick specified for the same job. And there is a genuine aesthetic beauty to glass bottle walls that allow light to permeate through them, with a delicate interplay of shape and colour that creates a great dynamic with the solidity of the wall in which they are set. It is a real skill to achieve such an effect that delivers a realisation of the amazing capacity for 'rubbish' to be turned into something inspiring.

Figure 74: Conservatory floor at Earthship Brighton made from reclaimed granite and marble off-cuts

Reclaimed timber and salvaged masonry are also used in earthships wherever possible. Earthship Brighton benefited from using the Brighton and Hove Wood Recycling Project for all the doors and floorboards used in construction. The Wood Recycling Project states that "every day a huge amount of waste timber is generated by industries working in construction, demolition and manufacture, wooden packaging waste and non-returnable pallets. Brighton and Hove Wood Recycling Project aims to rescue, reuse and recycle some of the tonnes of wood going to landfill locally by collecting waste wood from local businesses".[6.13] They then sold the timber they collected to clients such as Earthship Brighton who were happy to aid in the process of finding a use for a material that had been discarded and might have otherwise been consigned to landfill.

Stone is another material that is often discarded at various stages of its lifetime in construction, including at the induction stage when it is first assimilated from the quarry site. Even at this primary phase there is waste in the form of offcuts that do not quite make the quality control grade. The Earthship Brighton build benefited from a donation of end-of-vein offcuts of this type; in this case Portland stone from the company Albion Stone. This was used for the meeting room, kitchen and bathroom floors. Reclaimed granite offcuts from a local stonemason were used in a mosaic style for the hut and conservatory floor to make best use of the irregular shapes that had been sourced. Mosaic is a common style in earthship builds due to the fact that salvaged materials are often used in a best fit sense. There is a genuine design and craft skill to incorporating these materials into a build in a way that enhances the basic structure and functions of the earthship itself and creates a welcoming and comfortable environment for the inhabitants.

'JUNK AESTHETIC'

The sheer heterogeneity of material in earthships creates an unusual agglomeration of visual styles that could loosely be defined as a 'junk aesthetic'. That may sound like a pejorative term but the earthship is a building that deliberately makes use of, and indeed often makes beautiful, manufactured materials that have been dumped and discarded, as well as organic materials that have already been harvested and have been judged to have reached the end of their usefulness. It means that the reuse that occurs is twofold: firstly making use of the manmade materials that are so readily available, thus short circuiting the manufacturing process and reducing overall embodied energy, and secondly negating the need for direct harvesting of virgin natural materials such as timber by using reclaimed materials instead. The final visual result of this combination of materials might be seen as strange by some and a number of people describe the overall look as being 'post apocalyptic'. It should be remembered, though, that the underlying rationale behind the building is function and performance on human habitation and environmental criteria. The earthship forces us to re-examine aesthetics and the sense of what is beautiful in buildings mainly through its rootedness in performance and its direct connection with the natural elements. But it would also seem to be a strong argument that to build a self-sufficient, high performance home using many materials that have been rejected by the rest of society is, in itself, an immensely artistic and beautiful act.

CONCLUSION

Waste materials are not the only materials that are used in earthship construction. Inevitably, the greater part of the specification does involve newly manufactured products that are needed to make the earthship the high performance structure that it is aspiring to be. This means that some items have to be of extremely high grade specification, such as the photovoltaic panels, the glass and the insulation. These are all absolutely crucial to the performance of the building and it is impossible to compromise on them without compromising the very nature of the earthship itself. However, the waste products that are used are massively significant in terms of the overall resource outlook of the building and, indeed, as a provocation to the rest of the construction industry and society as a whole. The provocation is the statement 'look what can be done with what we throw away every day' and it is arguably a major part of what can be learned from earthships – that 'rubbish' can be useful.

The most obviously useful waste material in earthship construction is definitely the reused tyres. Thanks to the pioneer earthship builds in the UK, the regulatory position for building with this highly effective waste material is now much clearer, though still in need of supportive legislation. As a consequence of the lobbying that came out of the Earthship Brighton build, though, there is the hope that the necessary amendment to paragraph 19 of the 1994 legislation will provide this support. In the meantime there is the likely assurance that earthship builds will continue to be regarded by the Environment Agency as a low risk activity and assessed accordingly.

REFERENCES AND NOTES

[6.1] WRAP – for used tyre statistics see: www.wrap. org.uk/construction/tyres/dti_used_tyre_statistics/ index.html.

[6.2] Reynolds M (1990). Earthship Volume 1: How to build your own. Taos, New Mexico, Solar Survival Press, p77.

[6.3] Reynolds M (1990). Earthship Volume 1: How to build your own. Taos, New Mexico, Solar Survival Press, p78.

[6.4] WRAP statement (2006). Press office statement to the author, Kevin Telfer.

[6.5] For details of the Landfill Tax Credit Scheme and its objects see: www.ltcs.org.uk.

[6.6] The Guardian (November 19, 2006). 'Smart' homes to eat their rubbish.

[6.7] www.britglass.org.uk/Education/Recycling.html.

[6.8] Architects' Journal (19 June 2003). Earth mover (a profile of Mike Reynolds) by Kevin Telfer, pp18 –19.

[6.9] BRE (2006). Domestic energy factfile. Download from http://projects.bre.co.uk/factfile/ TenureFactFile2006.pdf.

[6.10] AJ Specification (August 2006). Specifier's choice/Earthship Brighton.

[6.11] Environment Council (2004). Required exemptions to waste management licensing for tyre recovery.

[6.12] Mike Reynolds M (1990). Earthship Volume 2: Systems and components. Taos, New Mexico, Solar Survival Press.

[6.13] www.woodrecycling.org.uk.

Earthship Brighton sunspace; floor and greywater planter wall made from reclaimed granite and adobe walls

CHAPTER 7
CONSTRUCTION METHODS

INTRODUCTION

This chapter outlines the build process of an earthship and explores the different stages of construction with the elements that comprise the building fabric. The story begins with the site selection and then builds the earthship from the ground up, starting with excavation and ramming the tyre walls, through to the installation of the water systems and final interior finishes. Some of the more conventional techniques and materials are not expanded on here. Throughout this chapter the main experience related is from the construction of Earthship Brighton; however, details of Earthship Fife

are included as well. Both demonstration projects are briefly summarised at the end of the chapter.

SITE SELECTION AND GROUND PREPARATION

Earthships are rammed tyre 'earth sheltered' timber framed buildings. They can be built on any south facing land, whether flat or a hillside. With a hillside site, such as in the construction of Earthship Brighton and Earthship Fife, the footprint of the building is excavated into the slope and the soil is piled in front

Figure 75: Site excavation and preparation for Earthship Brighton

of the building. If the soil has a clay consistency then it should be covered and kept dry. With a flat site the walls are rammed and then a backfill berm or earth shelter is moved to bury the walls of the building. The south facing aspect of the site should be completely unobstructed to maximise the solar gain or direct sunlight that can enter the building and be stored in the thermal mass walls and this requirement could limit the deployment of earthships in towns and cities. Ideally in the UK, the earthship should face slightly to the east to increase the penetration of the morning sun.[7.1]

Any excavated material from the site will be used later to pound the tyres and for backfill behind the tyres to create the berm or extra thermal mass. The rammed tyres and walls have a depth of around 2 m, the tyres on average being 700 mm in depth. The use of onsite soil keeps the transportation of heavy materials for the walls down, as only the used tyres need taking to the site. The damp proof membrane is installed underneath where the base of the wall is going to be built before the tyres are used to construct it. The width of the wall, coupled with the earthship being built on undisturbed ground, means that no foundation is required.

TYRE WALLS – METHODOLOGY

Used car tyres are effectively used to replace loadbearing masonry. The tyres are rammed or pounded a course at a time, up to 10 or 14 courses high. When fully rammed, each course is 250 mm high and each is staggered back 25 mm to retain the earth cliff or berm behind it. Each course is backfilled to the level of each completed course of tyres throughout the wall construction, which beds-in the tyres and provides stability. Once backfilled, the tyre walls are very stable as each tyre weighs over 50 kg; the weight of the rammed tyre means they are best worked on in position. The base of the rammed tyre also becomes 'shaped' to fit the area it is residing in. The first course can be partially filled with sand to protect any damp proof membrane underneath it. If necessary the tyres can be further reinforced by 'pinning' every two or tree tyres with metre-long stakes of a 12 mm reinforcing bar.

This method of tyre construction can also be used for a variety of other structural or non-structural applications, such as the footing for the front two

glass faces or straw bale builds. Potentially, any wall could be replaced with a rammed tyre wall, although the depth of the wall can restrict deployment of the technique.

After the first course the tyres are double lined with waste cardboard to cover the hole in the middle and filled with earth, each tyre taking two to three wheelbarrow loads to fill. The earth is compacted in a circular motion using a sledgehammer to pound the whole tyre equally until it is fully 'inflated' as solid thermal mass and levelled with itself and the adjacent tyres. If the tyre is over inflated it can be pounded back down or if under inflated can be pounded up to reach the desired level. Each tyre takes between 20 to 45 minutes to ram and any type of earth can be used, from chalk to clay as well as hardcore and other building rubble. It is a very labour intensive process. Earthship Brighton used 900 tyres or 9 tonnes of tyres of different sizes – 230 in the hut module and 670 in the nest – and took approximately 450 hours to manually ram. Earthship Fife used approximately 320 tyres. Tyre pounding is an example of a low skill activity that lots of volunteers can be used for and at the moment tyres are free; in the future people may be paid to take them away.

The tyres are laid like bricks, with a string line, and levelled. When finished they form virtually indestructible steel belted rubber walls. As the tyres are round they lend themselves to building undulating curves and other flowing organic shapes, but after packout they are equally good for creating straight walls. Between the tyre wall and the thermal wrap insulation layer, up to 1.5 m of earth is compacted to create extra thermal mass and to earth shelter the building.[7.1] Rigid insulation boards of 50 to 100 mm make up the thermal wrap behind the mass, isolating the walls from the ground behind the building. A tanking membrane then runs behind the insulation to completely encapsulate the earthship. In Earthship Brighton triple layered Visqueen 1200 gauge heavy duty plastic was used to damp proof the nest module and Rawell Environmental's Rawmat was used to tank the round hut module. Rawmat is bentonite clay sandwiched between two geotextile layers.

Figure 76: Tyre store (Earthship Brighton)

Figure 77: First course of tyres being laid on a damp proof course (Earthship Brighton)

Figure 78: Filling first course of tyres with sand to protect the damp proof course (Earthship Brighton)

Figure 79: Working on the seventh nest tyre wall (Earthship Brighton)

Figure 80: Installation of battery box thermal wrap insulation (Earthship Brighton)

Figure 81: Building the tyre walls of the hut module (Earthship Brighton)

SUITABILITY OF TYRES

There are a number of issues surrounding the suitability of using rammed tyres in construction: namely risk of fire, long term durability and leachate of hazardous chemical components.[7.2] Piles of discarded tyres have a high combustion risk as oxygen can freely flow through the structure, an example of which is the Heyope tyre dump near Knighton, Powys in Wales which is home to over 10 million used tyres and has been slowly smouldering since 1989.[7.3] However, the use of tyres in earthships is completely different as the tyres are rammed full of earth and rendered over with up to 25 mm of render. Therefore, oxygen is unable to circulate between the tyres, rendering the risk of fire as minimal. There is a notable example of rammed tyre earthship walls in a construction in the USA that survived a forest fire whilst the timber frame part of the building was destroyed.[7.4]

The possibility of leachate into the ground or groundwater from rammed tyres in construction is very low if the tyre wall is adequately damp proofed. Tyres are inert unless exposed to ultraviolet light, water or high temperature and the risk of this can be minimalised through tanking and rendering the tyres. There are various university studies in the USA that explore aspects of this subject.[7.5] While there have been no specific studies on the longevity or long term durability of tyres if they are protected from the elements that degrade them, anecdotal evidence would suggest they would last a very long time. There are earthships in New Mexico that have been standing for over 30 years.

TYRE SIZING AND ALTERNATIVE TYRE TECHNIQUES

Used car and van tyres come in many different sizes and performance varies when rammed with earth. Each tyre has a code on the side which is a description of it characteristics, for example 195/60/ R16 82 H. Table 14 summarises the numbers.

Although there can be other markings, tyre section width, aspect ratio/profile, and rim diameter are the only important considerations. Load index and speed rating are irrelevant in terms of the construction of tyre walls. The only other stipulation is that the tyre must not have a hole in it or be worn through. This means that 'old' tyres stockpiled in tyre dumps could be used as well as those recently disposed.

Generally, the most common tyre size in the UK is 195s of various diameters. A smaller tyre holds less earth, is lighter and therefore is more difficult to work as it moves around during the ramming process. In a tyre wall it is possible to use a variety of tyre sizes, but it is easier to use one uniform size as the tyres are laid evenly like bricks ie the middle of each tyre covers over the gap between the two tyres in the course below. If a variety of sizes are used then the larger tyres should be used at the bottom and the smaller ones towards the top. Even if care is taken it is likely that the wall may need additional techniques to fill any uneven gaps. The two main techniques are 'squeezies' and 'half block' pours. Squeezies are empty tyres forced into the void between two rammed tyres. The squeezy is then filled and rammed as normal. Half block pours involve creating formwork with a plasterer's lathe or wood around the hole that needs to be filled, and then a small pour of cement or other material to fill the gap. Half block pours can also be used to create vertical wall ends instead of tapering the tyre walls down to the ground.

Table 14: Tyre sizing

Component	Unit of measurement	Example
Tyre section width	mm	195
Aspect ratio/profile*	%	60
Cross-ply or radial construction	C or R	R
Diameter of rim	Inches	1
Load index	–	82
Speed rating	Letter	H

*The aspect ratio is the height of the section expressed as a percentage of the tyre section width.

WALL CONSTRUCTION

Tables 15 and 16 refer to the building material used for the construction of the walls in the nest and hut module for Earthship Brighton.

Table 15: Wall construction breakdown: Earthship Brighton nest module

Material component	Thickness (mm)	Lambda* (W/m²K)	R (m²k/W)
Surface R$_{se}$	–	–	0.13
Adobe plaster finish	13	0.570	0.023
Earth rammed tyres, pack out and rammed earth*	2000	1.000	2.000
Yelofoam X2i	100	0.029	3.448
Visqueen 1200 × 3 heavy gauge plastic	3	1.000	0.003
Surface R$_{si}$	–	–	0.04
Total	–	–	5.644
U-value for wall (W/m²K)	–	–	0.21

*The thickness for the pack out varies considerably. As the tyres are round this was difficult to calculate, therefore the walls have been calculated as if the tyres were flat and the mud render is just the finish. Calculation made using BRE U-value calculator.[7.6]

Table 16: Wall construction breakdown: Earthship Brighton hut module

Material component	Thickness (mm)	Lambda* (W/m²K)	R (m²k/W)
Surface R$_{se}$	–	–	0.13
Adobe plaster finish	13	0.570	0.023
Earth rammed tyres, pack out and rammed earth*	2000	1.000	2.000
Yelofoam X2i	100	0.029	3.448
Rawell Environmental Rawmat	5	1.000	0.002
Surface R$_{si}$	–	–	0.04
Total	–	–	5.644
U-value for wall (W/m²K)	–	–	0.21

*The thickness for the pack out varies considerably. As the tyres are round this was difficult to calculate, therefore the walls have been calculated as if the tyres were flat and the mud render is just the finish. Calculation made using the BRE U-value calculator.[7.6]

Footnote to Table 18
*Data provided and validated by manufacturer, in some cases tested or certified by 3rd party. U-values calculated using BuildDesk U Version 3.2.[7.7]

ROOF CONSTRUCTION

Table 17 and 18 refer to the building material used for the construction of the roofs in the nest and hut module for Earthship Brighton.

Table 17: Roof construction breakdown: Earthship Brighton nest module

Material component	Thickness (cm)	Lambda* (W/m²K)	R (m²K/W)
Surface R$_{se}$			0.04
CA 32 1000r steel profile roof	0.20	17.000	0.00
Tyvek Supro roofing membrane	0.00	0.100	0.00
Hard Rock dual density board	3.00	0.039	0.77
18 mm CDX ply deck	0.18	0.090	0.20
Rockwool Roll**	600.00	0.176	13.64
Visqueen 1200 heavy gauge plastic	0.00	0.330	0.00
6 mm birch ply	0.60	0.090	0.07
Surface R$_{si}$	–	–	0.10
Total	603.98	–	14.82
U-value for roof (W/m²K)	–	–	0.07*

*Data provided and validated by manufacturer, in some cases tested or certified by 3rd party.
**Roof trusses are 6 m long with a 4° pitch. The depth of insulation varies between 400 to 800 mm. The figure used is the average.

Table 18: Roof construction breakdown: Earthship Brighton hut module

Material component	Thickness (cm)	Lambda* (W/m²K)	R (m²K/W)
Surface R$_{se}$	–	–	0.04
Flagon EP/PR TPO single ply membrane	0.12	0.250	0.06
18 mm exterior grade ply deck	0.18	0.130	0.14
Xtratherm Thin-R pitched roof board	5.00	0.025	2.00
18 mm CDX ply deck	0.18	0.130	0.14
200 mm Rockwool Roll	20.00	0.088	4.54
Visqueen 1200 heavy gauge plastic	0.00	0.330	0.00
6 mm birch ply	0.60	0.090	0.07
Surface R$_{si}$	–	–	0.13
Total	26.08	–	7.12
U-value for roof (W/m²K)	–	–	0.14

ADOBE ABODE – TYRE RENDERING PREPARATION AND PACK OUT

After the tyre walls have been completed the walls are ready to be packed out to create a flat, easy-to-render surface. Although this usually happens after the roof structure is in place, the process will be described here to provide continuity in the discussion of tyre wall techniques. The material used for packout varies between internal and external tyre walls. Inside the material can be cob or mud, but exterior material must be waterproof, so that could be cement, eco-cement or an equivalent.

The voids between the adjacent tyres are filled with one handful of material and then a small bottle or can. Bottles and cans can be used to save on the volume of material used, although aluminium cans should be avoided and recycled, due to the high embodied of energy in aluminium. The voids can be 'porcupined' with nails before starting to create a better surface for the pack out material to adhere to. Pack out is repeated until all the voids are filled and then they are left to dry. The process is repeated and the next layer involves another handful of material with two bottles. After this a thin layer of scratch coat render should be applied to create a level surface for the final finished coat. All service infrastructure, plumbing and wiring, should be installed before the last coat. Adobe is mixed from clay, sand, topsoil and chopped straw obtained locally; the option of buying premixed adobe is very expensive.

Figure 82: Rammed tyre wall packout (Earthship Fife)

Figure 83: Attaching timber roof structure to wall plate and rammed tyre wall (Earthship Brighton)

FLOORS AND FOUNDATIONS

The footing for the front loadbearing faces can be constructed from rammed tyres or poured as a conventional footing, plated in a similar way to the other tyre wall then the front timber frame is attached. Two courses should be sufficient for this.

Once footings are in place the floor slab can be poured. The Earthship Brighton slab is a 100 mm eco-cement slab over Visqueen 1200 heavy gauge plastic blinded with sand on top of undisturbed chalk. Earthship Fife's slab was poured with limecrete. In Earthship Brighton and Earthship Fife there is no under floor insulation. The Earthship Brighton project experimented with eco-cement for rendering, pack out and other non-structural

applications, including the entire floor slab which throughout were poured with this material. Eco-cement is the invention of the Tasmanian John Harrison and uses magnesium and a pozzolan to replace two thirds of the ordinary Portland cement in a mix; this reduces the amount of cement needed to a third. Reactive magnesia has a lower embodied energy than cement, however it is difficult to source in the UK at the moment. Pozzolans can be easily obtained from a variety of sources.

Figure 84: Pouring eco-cement floor slab (Earthship Brighton)

Figure 86: Sloped front face timber wall plate (Earthship Brighton)

TIMBER FRAME CONSTRUCTION AND GLAZING

After the final course of tyres has been rammed the next step is to create a ring beam or wall plate secured to the walls with reinforcing bar to attach the roof structure to. The ring beam can be poured with concrete or can be a wooden wall plate; in Earthship Brighton the beam is a 300 × 50 mm pressure treated timber wall plate and the insulation 'thermal wrap' and damp proof course meet the beam and effectively seal the berm or mass behind the earthship. Now the rest of the timber frame part of the building can be erected. From this point all of the techniques are fairly standard, other than the occasional detail connecting the timber to the tyres, and follow the pattern of a conventional build. Once the front timber frames, roof trusses and structure are erected and the windows are fitted, the basic shell is completed and interior fit-out can begin.

Figure 87: Conservatory timber frame under construction (Earthship Brighton)

Figure 85: Attaching the nest wall plate to rammed tyres (Earthship Brighton)

Figure 88: Vertical timber face construction (Earthship Brighton)

Figure 89: Roof structure (Earthship Brighton)

Figure 90: Preliminary greywater planter wall preparation (Earthship Brighton)

WATER SYSTEMS INSTALLATION

The rainwater storage tanks are installed as the tyre walls are rammed, enabling them to be buried at the same time as the area behind the walls is backfilled. There are various options for rainwater tanks ranging from purpose made plastic tanks, ferro cement tanks to recycled orange juice containers. The vortex filter for pre-filtering rainwater can be installed at the same time as the tanks, but the bed of gravel is built after the framework and roof is finished. The water organising module can be fitted at the same time as the rest of the plumbing fixtures and once installed the supply side of the water systems are complete.

Once the front frames are in place and the floor slab has been poured the greywater planters can be built. The planters can be either a trough dug into the ground, a masonry wall built to retain the 'raised bed' or a combination of these. The trough is created to the required depth and prepared with sand to protect the damp proof membrane. The trench is lined with an ethylene propylene diene monomer (EPDM) rubber membrane, which is attached to sides and then the edges are rendered over to them. Another membrane can be placed inside as well to protect the EPDM membrane from any sharp gravel or stones. Next the plumbing fixtures are installed and rock bulbs are created around all pipe fittings, which will facilitate fast draining into and between

planters. Once all the bulbs are in place, the planter is filled with 20 mm gravel to the level the greywater will reach, up to 75 mm of sand and 150 mm of topsoil as the final layer. A grease and particle filter can then installed as outlined in chapter 5, and the plants should be planted last to avoid damage or dust. Once the plants are in place is takes several months for the eco-system that cleans the water to develop. The septic tank or other blackwater system can be installed towards the end of the project. Once the septic tank is in the water treatment side of the earthship is complete and the water systems can be used.

NATURAL VENTILATION

The earthship ventilation system relies on convection created between low set windows at the front of the building at ground and skylights at the back of the roof. To ventilate the building the gravity fed skylights are opened to exhaust unwanted heat which rises out and draws in cool air to replace it. In Earthship Brighton the skylights are Ubbink clear triple skin polycarbonate domes. The advantage of this ventilation system is that it enables the earthship to lose a lot of heat very rapidly during the day when it is hot in the summer months or to change the air very quickly in winter. In winter this method of ventilation can lead to heat loss, although a mechanical heat recovery system could overcome this. In Earthship Brighton there are two Monodraught Monovent sunpipes which act as passive stack vents to change the air in the kitchen and bathroom. This additional ventilation in the kitchen has the added bonus of dramatically increasing the level of natural daylight in a dark area of the building. The earthship ventilation system

Figure 91: Gravity-fed skylight locked shut with clam cleat (Earthship Brighton)

Figure 92: Open skylights (Earthship Brighton)

could be easily modified to draw cool air in from under a wooden deck for even more effective cooling in summer.

MATERIAL SPECIFICATION

Low impact and natural materials

The two projects that have been completed in the UK both benefited from a large supply of voluntary labour, which has enabled them to prepare a range of salvaged and reclaimed materials. It is likely that if the cost of these activities were factored in the cost would be prohibitive, for example de-nailing and sanding reclaimed timber from skips. Earthship Brighton used 2 t cans/bottles, 1500 cardboard boxes, reclaimed timber including elm, oak cladding and 150 m reclaimed floorboards, 90 salvaged granite blocks, 5 t granite off-cuts and 35 reclaimed paving slabs. At the moment it remains far cheaper to purchase new materials in volume than preparing second hand materials and crafting them into the build process.

BOTTLE WALLS AND GLASS BRICKS

The first step to building a bottle wall is to measure the size of the bottle wall, to get the length of the glass bricks needed and help calculate the number needed to fill the space. For this calculation a gap of 25 mm should be left between each course and between each brick. Next the bottles can be collected and grouped in terms of size and colour; two bottles of the same diameter are needed for one glass brick. Using a wet tile cutter, the bottles are cut to half the length of the glass brick, with the neck half being discarded, glass dust is extremely hazardous and adequate precautions should be taken at all times. The bottom halves are then cleaned and when dry are taped together with gaffer tape to make one glass brick. For a deep colour two bottles of the same colour can be used or for a lighter shade a clear bottle can be taped to a coloured bottle, when used the clear end should be on the sunny side. The glass bricks are then laid in courses, leaving a minimum of 25 mm between bottles with no more than six courses being laid a day. Once all the bricks have been laid they are rendered over and whilst the plaster is wet it is thoroughly cleaned with wet sponges and clothes to reveal the glass bottles beneath. Can walls can be built in a similar fashion, but the cans are used intact. There is one large bottle wall in the bathroom and two small walls in the office and meeting room of Earthship Brighton, while Earthship Fife demonstrates the technique as a finishing around a door.

PLAN VIEW AND ROOM SPECIFICATION

Earthship Fife – project overview

The Earthship Fife project began in 2000 after Paula Cowie returned from a holiday in Taos, New Mexico visiting earthships. Sustainable Communities Initiatives was then set up with the

Table 19: Earthship Fife room dimensions

Room	Length/diameter (m)	Width (m)	Area (m²)
Office	6.00	5.25	31.50
Total	–	–	31.50

aim of determining if the concept would work in the Scottish climate, how the planning authorities would receive it and how much it would cost.

A south facing site on Craigencalt Farm was found and it was decided that Earthship Fife would form part of the already established Craigencalt Ecology Centre. After receiving a building warrant the initial construction phase began in July 2002 with a training programme for 10 trainees provided by experienced builders from the USA, including Mike Reynolds. During one week the basic structure was completed, and the remaining building work was carried out at

Figure 93: Earthship Fife visitor centre opening

weekends and on volunteer days until the building was launched in 2004. The earthship is just over 6 × 5 m approximately 31 m², comprising over 300 tyres, 1500 cans, reclaimed timber and other natural products including sheep's wool insulation, clay membranes and earth plaster.

The Earthship Fife visitor centre was launched in August 2004 and in 2005 the Sustainable Communities Initiatives won the Vision in Business of the Environment of Scotland award in the small company category. The thermal dynamics and design of the building have proven that the earthship concept does work in the Scottish climate. During winter the internal temperature has not fallen below 12°C, so very little back up heating has been needed. Unfortunately, the original roof design did not work and was changed in 2006 due to reoccurring dampness problems. The whole project is described in detail in the Earthship toolkit.[7.5]

Earthship Brighton – project overview

The Earthship Brighton project began in 2000 with the creation of the Low Carbon Network (LCN) by various interested parties in Brighton. The LCN was formed to highlight the connection of buildings and climate change through innovative demonstration projects and communications work. Earthship Brighton was the LCN's first initiative and is a community centre for Stanmer Organics, a Soil

Table 20: Earthship Brighton room dimensions

Room (m)	Length/ diameter	Width (m)	Area (m²)
Meeting room	10.00	6.00	60.00
Conservatory	11.50	2.50	28.75
Kitchen	3.60	3.60	13.00
Bathroom	2.50	2.50	6.25
Office	4.00	-	12.50
Total	-	-	120.50

Figure 94: Meeting room (Earthship Brighton)

Box 5

EARTHSHIP BRIGHTON: TIMELINE

April 2000: Earthship pioneer Mike Reynolds, gives a presentation to 150 people at the Brighthelm Centre in Brighton.

July 2000: The Low Carbon Network (LCN) is founded by people and various local organisations in Brighton and Hove to build the first Earthship in England.

August 2000: A suitable site identified at Stanmer Organics, Stanmer Park, offering synergy with existing land based projects to build a community centre for environmental education.

January 2001: Earthship preliminary design worked up by Clifton Design and submitted for planning permission by Brighton Permaculture Trust.

September 2001: City Councillors grant draft planning permission.

December 2001: Low Carbon Network incorporates, becoming Low Carbon Network Ltd.

January 2002: Business plan and major funding applications are developed and submitted by C Level and Low Carbon Network.

February 2002: BOC Foundation supports Earthship Brighton.

March 2002: Biffaward in principle joins BOC with majority funding covering all phases of the project.

May 2002: LCN secures Environmental Body status from ENTRUST, the government regulator for landfill tax credits (Biffaward).

July 2002: Funding is fully confirmed from Biffaward and full planning permission is granted. Communication Work Group issues a joint press release with SCI who begin Earthship Fife. Well placed article in *The Guardian* gets front page leading to TV coverage and large scale awareness of Earthships in the UK.

July 2002: LCN team train on Fife project.

October 2002: First funding released and design work group starts on design phase.

Winter 2002: Design finalised and adapted to the UK climate. A member of the LCN build crew, George Clinton, trains on Earthship builds in Taos, New Mexico.

February 2003: Environment Agency takes exceptional step of giving authority to build Earthship Brighton using waste car tyres without the need for a waste management licence.

April 2003: Stanmer site in Brighton prepared and work begins.

May 2003: Mike Reynolds and crew come over to England to help build the hut module and train LCN crew in Earthship construction techniques.

June 2003: Partial ban of tyres from landfill across Europe under the European Landfill Directive.

Summer 2003: All tyres rammed. Timber frame and shell of Earthship is built and rainwater harvesting systems installed. Successfully start harvesting rainwater in August.

December 2003: After six months of building, financial issues stop construction of the project.

April 2004: University of Brighton 'Durabuild' programme begins a 3-year study into the thermal performance of Earthship Brighton and installs 32 temperature probes throughout the building.

August 2004: EDF Energy's 'Green Fund' helps support the cost of the renewable power systems.

Summer 2004: Earthship Brighton is weatherproofed and all the floor slabs are poured with eco-cement. This is the first use of this low carbon pioneering technology in the UK.

October 2004: International Earthship Summit is held at University of Brighton. 95 delegates attend from across Europe. Mosaic floors laid in conservatory and the 'hut' module.

November/April 2005: Two philanthropic societies lend support to the project.

Summer 2005: In the midst of a drought and hosepipe ban Earthship Brighton harvests over 20k litres of rainwater in 6 weeks during July and August.

October 2005: With DTI and Energy Saving Trust funding the 20 kW power systems are installed, including the first wind turbine in Brighton and Hove. Septic tank also installed.

November 2005: LCN wins the South East Renewable Sustainable Energy Awards for the Earthship Brighton project in the field of innovation.

June 2006: 3000th visitor given a tour. Earthship Brighton has been featured in over 60 articles and TV appearances.

July 2006: Tyres completely banned from landfill under the European Landfill Directive. Funding secured from British Gas to complete project.

August 2006: Rainwater purification system fitted. Water to be tested. Once up to a potable standard Earthship Brighton will be the first public building that uses rainwater for all activities, from bathing to drinking.

September 2006: Secretary of State for the Environment, Rt Hon David Miliband MP, visits Earthship Brighton.

December 2006: Last building phase and Earthship Brighton is completed. LCN becomes the Low Carbon Trust (LCT)

March 2007: LCT commended in the Environment Agency's water efficiency Awards in *Sustain* magazine's construction and renovation category and finalist in DfES category.

Spring 2007: 4 500th visitor given a tour and the project has been featured in over 110 mainstream media articles. A last volunteer push in June completed the landscaping of the surrounding grounds and built a blackwater treatment system.

June 2007: Earthship Brighton is the National Gold Winner of the 'Green Apple Award' for the built environment and architectural heritage in the new build tourism category.

Summer/Autumn 2007: Earthship Brighton sets sail and a book about the project *Earthships – Building a zero carbon future for homes* by IHS BRE Press is launched.

Association accredited organic co-operative, set in a 17 acre site, in Stanmer Park, near Brighton. The aim of the project was to successfully transfer earthship technology by building an earthship show home, in essence a model three bedroom dwelling in all but layout as a community facility.

It took the first couple of years to locate the land, get the earthship designed, obtain planning permission, resolve building control issues, raise funds from a variety of sources including the landfill tax credit scheme and adapt Mike Reynolds' design to be suitable to the temperate English climate.

Construction began in April 2003 with Mike Reynolds and his crew coming over from New Mexico for a week to build the hut module and train people to deliver the rest of the project. The rest of the tyre walls were constructed over the next couple of months and the shell of the earthship was completed by winter 2003. Due to the experimental nature of the project additional funds were required to complete the build and since 2003 short bursts of focused building activity have been facilitated by extra funds being raised.

The power systems were installed in October 2005, including the first wind turbine in Brighton and Hove and for the Earthship Brighton project the LCN won the South East Renewable Energy Awards in the category of Innovation. In 2006 the last funding needed to complete the project was secured from British Gas and the building was completed over a 6-week period in the autumn of 2006. The water recycling systems were installed and interior fit was completed. In 2007 the Low Carbon Network became the Low Carbon Trust and Earthship Brighton was opened to the public as a community centre in the summer. In March 2007 the Low Carbon Trust was commended in the Environment Agency's water efficiency awards in the Construction and Renovation category and in June 2007 won a Green Apple award.

REFERENCES AND NOTES

[7.1] Reynolds M (1990). Earthship volume 1: How to build your own. Taos, New Mexico, Solar Survival Press, pp44-46.

[7.2] See the Gaia research report on www.gaiagroup.org for a detailed analysis of the risks to tyres.

[7.3] www.guardian.co.uk/wastestory/0,12188, 747921,00.html.

[7.4] Reynolds, M (2001). Comfort in any climate. Taos, New Mexico, Solar Survival Press.

[7.5] Cowie P (2004). The earthship toolkit: Your guide to building a zero waste zero energy future. Kinghorn, Sustainable Communities Initiatives.

[7.6] BRE (2007). U-value calculator. Available from www.brebookshop.com.

[7.7] BuildDesk U version 3.2. www.builddesk. co.uk/graphics/BuildDesk_UK/ OUR_SOFTWARE/ BuildDesk_U/2_BD-data_U-UK.pdf.

Rear entrance to the Happy Castle at night (Taos, New Mexico)

CHAPTER 8
WHAT IS THE FUTURE OF EARTHSHIPS?

INTRODUCTION

For all the ground this book has covered the reality of the contemporary situation is that there are only two earthships that have been built in the UK and neither of them fulfils the primary intended use of earthships – as residential buildings. The paucity of earthships in this country has been noted by commentators such as Sutherland Lyall in *AJ Specification*. "Unlike proselytisers for many nice architectural ideas," he writes, "the promoters of earthships do not make wild claims. They do not say earthships are going to solve the current housing shortage… Nor will earthships solve the first-time buyer problem… Nor would earthships make a serious dent in the used car tyre mountain."[8.1] So if all this is true, what in fact is the relevance and importance of earthships in a UK context and what is going to be their future here? Well, Sutherland Lyall himself goes on to say that "nevertheless this first English example…has potentially important lessons for the design of sustainable architecture in general", and it is this that strikes at the heart of what is significant about earthships.[8.1] The earthship is as much as anything a provocation at a time when the architectural and building communities in the UK most require provocation. On almost every tenet of sustainability in construction it provides an example of what can be achieved and what more could be achieved with significant investment and political will. This has enormous relevance at a juncture when sustainable living, of which architecture is a significant part, is arguably the greatest – and most urgent – challenge facing society in general as the potentially catastrophic consequences of climate change become truly apparent.

This chapter looks in detail at how the earthship provides a lead both for the zero carbon sustainable housing revolution that needs to take place in the UK and for the retrofitting of existing building stock.

It also examines the design trajectory of future earthship builds in the UK and how they might benefit from the experience of the initial prototypes, as well as the chances of large numbers of earthships being built, both as major developments and self-builds, in this country.

EARTHSHIPS AS PROVOCATIVE AGENTS OF CHANGE

A 'nice architectural idea' may not be the most apt description of an earthship, a structure that is seen by some in the architectural profession as an ugly carbuncle that should be sent back across the Atlantic and consigned to the desert of New Mexico forever. But the earthship is not a building that is trying to fit in. It is emblematic of a new paradigm that has to become increasingly prevalent not just in the UK but globally, if there is to be a genuine effort on the part of mankind to drastically reduce carbon emissions into the atmosphere and to live more sustainably in general. The earthship also offers an architectural alternative to human alienation from the natural world which is embodied in the majority of present housing; an alienation which in itself is arguably the cause of much of the environmental damage being wreaked on the planet. In both these senses earthships point towards a necessary future for architecture.

The earthship is a performance based sustainable structure that needs to deliver all the basic comforts and amenities to its inhabitants because it does not have the back up of being connected to infrastructure. This divorce from centralised utilities means that the building has to have well developed survival strategies. These are not without flaws, as we will see later in this chapter, but the UK earthships offer a showcase for these strategies and concepts, many of which will need to be used in various forms by other zero carbon sustainable new builds in this country.

What follows is a rundown of the individual aspects of UK earthships that provoke, provide inspiration, and offer a testing ground and a challenge for architects, developers and building professionals alike.

ZERO CARBON HOMES

'Zero carbon building' is becoming a truly zeitgeist phenomenon, an anthem in print and sound bites. The architectural press is saturated with zero carbon stories ('zero carbon is becoming mainstream' wrote head of sustainability at the Building Design Partnership, Trevor Butler, in *Building Design Magazine* in January 2007)[8.2] and certain parts of the government seem very enthusiastic about zero carbon homes. The need to reduce carbon emissions in order to try and slow down the runaway train that is climate change is also acknowledged by many key figures in the construction industry. But as this book goes to press there nonetheless remains a scarcity of projects on the ground that are actually demonstrating the principle of a zero carbon build. Brighton and Fife can offer an inspiration in practical terms along with some of the few other pioneer sustainable building projects such as BedZED for how to achieve this goal. This inspiration may be seen as being particularly powerful because of the grassroots nature of the Earthship Brighton and Earthship

Figure 95: David Miliband, as the then secretary of state for the environment, visited Earthship Brighton in 2006, pictured with Mischa Hewitt

Fife builds that show what can be achieved with relatively few organisational and structural resources. However, the earthship is also a reminder that other sustainability goals as well as zero carbon can, and should, be incorporated into zero carbon buildings.

SITE HARMONY AND ONE PLANET LIVING

The idea that a building cannot only function adequately by solely using the resources that are available to it onsite, but in a way that provides comfortable living for its inhabitants, is a challenging one for architects and developers. This also relates to the point below on the problems with centralised infrastructure. The earthship uses abundant site-available renewable natural resources to the building's maximum advantage with minimal impact to the environment through a number of sustainable strategies that make best use of the elements, particularly the sun, but also the wind and the rain. This means that the building has a one planet eco-footprint that negates the insatiable thirst for energy, water and other resources that is the present unsustainable norm for most housing. The earthship provides ideas to designers and developers as to how this can be achieved and empowers householders with a connection to their natural environment, ownership of their building services and low running costs.

CRITIQUE OF INFRASTRUCTURE

It is highly unlikely for a number of reasons that more than a handful of the significant number of new homes being built over the next 20 years will be offgrid. Nonetheless, the earthship offers a very plausible alternative to the slavish reliance on centralised solutions that characterises our present housing. We have looked in this book at some of the problems associated with large scale infrastructure: principally that it is inefficient and has significant carbon emission and resource depletion problems associated with it. Infrastructure has also effectively led to a dependence culture which means that our homes are, on their own, weak and vulnerable without their various connections. If, as is predicted, severe weather events become increasingly common due to climate change there will be more and more disruption to central infrastructure-supplied utilities in times of drought, floods and high winds. The earthship suggests a housing model that at the very least significantly reduces its dependence on grid based solutions so that it can more effectively self-deliver space heating through passive solar and thermal mass, self-provide clean water with rainwater harvesting and filtration and self-generate electricity from whatever source is most suited to the site. That also means that running costs are negligible, which could, perhaps, provide a solution for the weak and vulnerable in society who are at risk from extremes of heat and cold and cannot afford the energy hungry means of ameliorating extreme temperature through either air conditioning or heating. Whether these people will be able to afford to live in such a home, though, is a question for developers, housing associations and local authorities.

BUILDING WITH WASTE AND LOW EMBODIED ENERGY MATERIALS

Anecdotally it seems that the most provoking thing about earthships to many people is the fact that they use old car tyres as an integral part of their construction. This is not just a provocation to the building industry but to the whole of society in terms of demonstrating the potential usefulness of many materials, such as tyres, that are simply thrown away each day and considered waste. This also forms a strong critique of the wastefulness that is endemic in the majority of developed countries such as the UK and throws down the gauntlet of re-use. And the construction lesson here is centred on using low embodied energy materials wherever possible. Through the first UK earthship builds' exploration of the legislative and regulatory framework, the opportunity for future builds to use similar techniques will benefit from a more certain knowledge of what is involved and possible. But the fact of building with tyres also captures something else about earthships – their innovative quirkiness and charisma. It could be argued that this design approach should serve as an inspiration to other designers of zero carbon buildings in terms of being open minded, performance driven and unafraid of trying something new. Tyres are certainly not used

gratuitously in earthships or even celebrated; they are simply integrated with the structural and thermal performance of the building and then vanish behind a veneer; a highly positive design solution. These are exciting times for zero carbon design and there are significant opportunities for incorporating high performance standards in new forms of architectural expression to create similarly charismatic buildings.

DEMAND REDUCTION AND RENEWABLE SUPPLY

Demand reduction is the first step in making all resource pathways sustainable, as amply demonstrated in earthships. The second step is ensuring that supply is from renewable sources and that it is capable of matching the real need that does exist. The overwhelming focus in earthships of making use of resources such as the sun for passive solar heating is emblematic of numerous strategies to try and keep occupant demand for utilities as low as possible. This is an expression of the idea of site harmony discussed above. Instead of the paradigmatic crisis at present of most housing failing to take anything significant from encounters with the elements, the earthship provides inspiration by illustrating how buildings can easily benefit from harnessing what is useful from the sun, wind and rain. This not only finds its expression in demand reduction but on the supply side as well, with microgenerative technologies making use of the energy potential of the sun and wind, and rainwater harvesting supplying the occupants with fresh water.

PASSIVE SOLAR, THERMAL MASS AND THERMAL PERFORMANCE

The major form of demand reduction employed by the earthship and other zero carbon buildings is that of passive solar heating, thermal mass and super insulation that massively reduces the conventional space heating requirement, which on average forms just under 60% of domestic UK energy consumption by end use. The earthship offers one model of these principles in action and the Earthship Brighton and Earthship Fife demonstration projects offer good opportunities to examine the efficacy of the approach taken. For any zero carbon building in a temperate climate to achieve its aspiration cutting heat demand is the most fundamental factor to get right; it is therefore worthy of significant study. It should be noted, though, that other models, eg super insulation combined with sustainable space heating such as biomass combined heat and power, may also be able to supply the same end result of effective renewable thermal performance without solar orientation, although there are other factors involved here eg carbon implications of biomass transport.

WATER HARVESTING AND RECYCLING

The likelihood is that due to the consequences of climate change not only will there be more drought in the future, but more unpredictable weather in general that will feature very intense rain. The Environment Agency Sustainable Development Unit said in June 2001 that "major floods that have only happened before say, every 100 years on average, may now start to happen every 10 or 20 years".[8.3] In these conditions, homes that have the capacity for water storage will benefit from being able to harvest water at such times of intense rainfall conditions for use when the resource may be scarce. Given the recent history of drought, particularly in certain areas of the UK, it would seem that innovation is required to try and ameliorate this growing problem. This is particularly the case in south east England where the main demand for new housing meets the historically worst hit area in the country for drought. The earthship offers a way forward in terms of its intensely economic use of water that does not drain the centralised supply at all. Once again it is a provocation to society in general, and to legislators in particular, about valuing a vital resource as well as an opportunity for testing the efficacy of the earthship harvesting and recycling systems in a UK environment.

It would seem, then, that earthships are extremely provocative and hard to ignore on a number of different fronts, while the integrated nature of their approach offers a compelling vision of where residential building may go in the next 20 years. Thus we can see the veracity of Sutherland Lyall's comment that earthships have "potentially important lessons for the design of sustainable architecture in general". Their relevance is as evolved models of sustainable building that have been developed over a period of 30 years and that now forms part of the (admittedly small) vanguard of zero carbon sustainable building in this country. It is likely that this vanguard will in turn form the basis of future residential sustainable models. In terms of the operation of various systems the present earthships also offer great opportunities for testing, eg with thermal performance, which will be of great use to future earthship and other sustainable builds.

The inevitable question of whether earthships are likely to become a widespread phenomenon in themselves (and if not, why not?) is looked at in more detail below.

HOME BUILDING IN THE UK – A REVOLUTION IN ZERO CARBON HOMES?

The particular relevance of earthships at this time is in large part due to the context of the sustainability debate, which is principally being driven by the increasingly alarming predictions of what impacts climate change is likely to have. As previously mentioned, the government-commissioned Stern review has been a major factor in pushing this debate into the mainstream and would also seem to be a significant driver for government action. And there have been significant announcements from government departments with the Code for Sustainable Homes as an improvement on BRE's BREEAM standard, the *Building a greener future: Towards zero carbon development* consultation document[8.4] and major planning changes all being proposed within a few weeks of the release of Sir Nicholas Stern's report at the end of October 2006. Three key ministers (Gordon Brown, Yvette Cooper and Ruth Kelly) all made the stated aspiration of all new homes being zero carbon by 2016 during a flurry of announcements in December 2006. One of the first fiscal measures to be proposed in order to incentivise zero carbon homes to the consumer is a stamp duty exemption on zero carbon rated homes from 2007.

Figure 96: BowZED in the east end of London is an exemplar of passive solar, passive ventilation and microgenerative residential design on a tightly constricted urban site. Could this be the future of zero carbon building in the UK?

As this book has set out, though, the aspiration and positive sentiment towards a zero carbon building future is clouded somewhat by the sheer demand for housing that exists in the UK. The government aim following Kate Barker's recommendations in 2004, *Delivering stability: securing our future housing needs. Barker review of housing supply*[8.5] is to increase the housing supply to 200 000 homes per year by 2016 through the Code for Sustainable Homes initiative (in 2004/05 168 000 homes were delivered). This means that overall carbon emissions will still increase despite significant improvements on individual home performance.

The other significant caveat to the December 2006 announcements is that the proposal for the Code for Sustainable Homes is for a voluntary code that may not be enforced through building standards. The consultation document states (clause 2.20) that "whilst a mandatory code rating would help drive better environmental standards, the Code is essentially a voluntary set of environmental standards – we are not proposing that any development or building should be required to meet those higher standards (except where public funding is involved)."[8.6] This is given further credence by the lobbying position of numerous groups such as the Home Builders Federation who argue that industry needs the 'space to deliver' the expected improvements in standards, which is essentially shorthand for urging the government to adopt a low regulation, market-driven attitude to delivering change. It would seem that the target is to achieve mandatory status for the Code by 2008, although the position would seem to be ambiguous and undecided. Any non-mandatory initiative, though, would seem to immediately compromise the targets that stand at an aim of a 25% improvement on Part L of the Building Regulations by 2010, a 44% improvement by 2013 and full zero carbon rating by 2016. The voluntary period of this proposal is ongoing as this book goes to press and it is not possible to fully assess its merits until (and if) it becomes mandatory and backed up with Building Regulations. At the time of writing there is also a consultation open on the future of zero carbon homes which may result in more definite proposals.[8.6]

However, if the stated government targets are taken at face value, there is a major manifesto for change and the government has effectively thrown down the gauntlet for architects and developers. The announcements seem to have been welcomed by many: co-founder of BioRegional, Sue Riddlestone, stated that she "was delighted that the government has taken this bold step",[8.7] and the president of RIBA Jack Pringle said that "taking new homes to zero carbon within ten years is an ambitious but necessary government target, and the Code for Sustainable Homes will be fundamental to meeting it. I am delighted that the government has responded to calls by RIBA and others to strengthen the Code, and I welcome the news of moves towards a mandatory approach for new homes alongside building regulation reform".[8.7] Trevor Butler, writing in *Building Design Magazine*, seemed to approve of the idea of a stamp duty exemption incentive. "This initiative certainly captures the imagination of the buying public and clients alike" he wrote. "Immediately after Gordon Brown's announcement last December a major commercial developer asked us (Building Design Partnership) to aim for 'zero carbon' status for a mixed-use London scheme."[8.2] Butler concedes that "the additional capital cost of opting for a zero carbon home is likely to outweigh the benefits of not paying stamp duty", but overall believes that the proposals are "a step in the right direction".[8.2]

It would seem that there are a significant number of major low or zero carbon developments under consideration, although there is little to see on the ground at the beginning of 2007. Of course, one of the difficulties is simply the fact that designing zero carbon homes uses emerging technologies and design ideas that have not been sufficiently tested as yet. This is where the earthship can be extremely effective in offering lessons to the new build market; it has evolved over a number of years of trial and error. There is also the need for a performance based visual aesthetic that incorporates all the necessary technologies for successful functioning of a home that will also need to be desirable and competitively priced on the new build market. In addition, for the kind of mass production required by the new build industry there also needs to be a cheap supply chain of appropriate materials in place as keeping the unit costs down as far as possible is of prime importance from a business perspective.

Unsurprisingly it does cost more to build to zero carbon standards as many of the specifications need to be superior to those that meet currently applicable lowest common denominator building standards. And that cost is significant due to the fact that it eats into profit, of course: the primary motive in all major home building. Butler's concern about additional capital costs involved in zero carbon homes outweighing the payback periods is a significant one, also relevant to earthships, particularly when much of the homes shortage in the UK is in the 'affordable homes' sector and also when we consider the major impact that bad housing can have on the most vulnerable people in society. Is zero carbon housing only going to be for the well off? The fact that the Peabody Trust was the developer at BedZED where 15 homes from 82 were at affordable rent for social housing suggests that not all of it will be.

EARTHSHIPS AS A MASS ZERO CARBON HOUSING SOLUTION

In the UK the concept of earthships solving the zero carbon housing shortage, as Sutherland Lyall has observed, is practically a non-starter for a number of reasons. The critical problems are those of cost and density taken together. Earthships are relatively low density and, perhaps counter intuitively given the amount of reclaimed materials involved, relatively expensive to build on flat sites (sloped sites generally result in lower construction costs and are also less desirable sites). This combination is the kiss of death in terms of the developer's profit margin and therefore the main reason why earthships will not get built in vast quantities in the UK. Where the housing demand is highest, in the south east of England, is where there is the least space and the greatest need for high density housing solutions. Land costs also require high density development. In addition, low density housing is not a good ecological solution as it increases transport and reduces the natural habitat. This density problem is an understandable result of the genesis of earthships in the relatively barren and absolutely vast spaces of the New Mexico desert where land can also be extremely inexpensive.

Density and cost issues, however, are not the only problems associated with earthship builds. The amount of manual labour involved in constructing earthships is fairly high, due in the main to the physically intensive process of ramming tyres and building walls with them. Both the Brighton and Fife builds used large number of volunteers that helped to drive the labour costs down, but this is obviously not a serious business proposition. The fact that the labour also uses new techniques that have to be learned onsite, such as tyre ramming, is a short-term impediment only as the skills are essentially easy to teach and quick to learn, while other onsite skill requirements such as joinery and plastering are similar to any other conventional build.

Lastly, there is the problem of negative perception among the architectural and construction industry that this book is a serious effort to dispel. That perception is largely due to the innovative and grassroots approach of earthship builders that arouses the suspicion that they are the work of some kind of lunatic fringe. It is the least significant of the problems faced due to the other factors being critical barriers to mass production of earthships. However, as this book has hopefully demonstrated, earthships are in fact well designed, serious buildings that can provoke and inspire the design and construction communities in the UK.

The more likely scenario of the future of earthships in the UK is that of a number of individual builds or small scale developments, where the client is committed to the values embodied by the earthship and is perhaps prepared to wait for the payback times to come back from the initial capital investment. It is likely that these payback times would exceed 10 years in earthships so that commitment would need to be genuinely long term in order to gain full benefit.

But there is another potential scenario for the future. This scenario is to employ all the sustainability measures used in earthships but to modify the design in order to increase density, drive down construction costs and facilitate lower labour requirements. Mike Reynolds has had the idea to stack earthships and it could be argued that a development like BedZED is not dissimilar in concept from the idea of stacked and terraced earthships with south facing passive solar glazing, thermal mass, passive ventilation, greenhouses and other sustainability measures including water harvesting and photovoltaic arrays. The Hockerton Housing Project also has generic similarities, particularly due to the fact that it is earth sheltered, while achieving a slightly higher density through a terracing approach. It should be remembered that performance is the key criterion for the earthship concept and using different materials to achieve that performance is desirable so long as the materials themselves do not have high embodied energy values. Rising to the challenges that have been identified should also be a way forward; earthships surely have to continue to evolve to suit the specific requirements demanded by the UK housing environment.

In a sense this comes down to the question 'when is an earthship not an earthship' ie how far does the concept have to be modified before it simply becomes a zero carbon sustainable home? It might be argued that high density in itself displaces the earthship paradigm that is essentially an ultimate statement of personal empowerment and North American individualism. The high density, community centred focus of BedZED arguably feels like communism in comparison! There is no simple answer to this question and in a way it is not important; the key factor is producing more sustainable zero carbon homes and if earthships can feed their strategies into this overall drive, however diffusely, then this has to be seen as a positive development.

FUTURE EARTHSHIP CONSTRUCTION – SPECIFIC BUILDS

There are a number of different earthship builds in various stages of development across the world. These include: a build that started in April 2007 in Normandy, France; a large residential earthship called the Phoenix that is under construction in New Mexico, USA; and a proposed earthship development at the Brighton marina in the UK. There are also numerous self-builds underway in the USA and anecdotal reports that other small scale projects in the UK are close to applying for planning permission.

The Phoenix earthship is a three bedroom, two bathroom home that also features huge interior growing areas for food production. This is a further expansion of the self-sufficiency premise and aims to be able to cultivate large amounts of food for the inhabitants using only recycled water and the sun that floods through the windows. It is a potential survival tool for a future in which food shortages due to climate change related drought may become commonplace. Mike Reynolds argues that "earthships

can make it so people can take care of themselves in an uncertain future. But if introduced in a large way soon enough, they can change that future."[8.8] He has also worked to get legislation passed in New Mexico whereby there is now an act for sustainable development test sites, "providing for the approval of areas to be used for non-industrial research and testing designed to reduce the consumption and dependence on natural resources by residential development".[8.8]

It would seem from the existing prototypes of UK earthships that modifications to the US design could be made to improve their performance. In particular there is not the same need for flat roofs in this country as there is in New Mexico where the roof captures snow melt in the winter. Snow is generally very infrequent in the UK and a more steeply sloping roof would enable water capture without the added risks that flat roofs bring. The relative lack of sunlight compared to New Mexico might also mean that other more economical microgeneration technologies need to be considered. The thermal performance testing that is ongoing at Earthship Brighton will be able to evaluate how other aspects of the building are performing in UK environmental conditions and enable tweaking for future builds if necessary.

At the time of going to press a 16-unit development in Brighton (called 'The Lizard' due to the fact that the site is also a habitat for lizards that the development aims to maintain and safeguard) was granted planning permission by Brighton and Hove City Council. The development will be a mix of one, two and three bedroom earthships and six will be available through a local housing association as affordable homes.

If built this will be a significant step forward for earthship building in the UK and follows a six month feasibility study that was jointly funded by the Environment Agency and the Energy Saving Trust. The developers, Earthship Biotecture state on their website that "Biotecture carried out the study in partnership with Brighton and Hove City Council and the Chichester Diocese Housing Association as well as architects and surveyors. The partnership found no barriers to small scale residential earthship colonies in the UK and earmarked the Brighton Marina site as potentially suitable for such a development."[8.9] The outcome of this development is of great interest both in terms of being the likely first residential earthships in the UK. The financial aspects of the project will make interesting reading for developers while the performance of residential buildings will enable a more accurate picture to be formed of the overall efficacy of earthships as residential buildings in a UK environment. After planning permission had been granted Martin Randall, Assistant Director of Planning for Brighton and Hove City Council stated that "The proposal occupies a site overlooking the Brighton Marina where the principle of housing along more traditional lines has been long established, but no scheme so far has been forthcoming. The Lizard development falls below national planning density targets (30 dwellings per hectare) but in this particular instance, the unique sustainability benefits have helped to inform a positive decision.

The earthship dwellings are distinctive and contrast with the existing built environment in terms of their design and an orientation which aims to maximise solar gain. Each earthship incorporates a wind turbine and photovoltaic panels are used to produce electricity. The development will not however, have an adverse impact on the character or appearance of the locality and responds positively to the new agenda for design. Effective monitoring will be a vital part of determining the effectiveness of different aspects of this sustainable design and their applicability to other schemes in the city."

EARTHSHIP SELF-BUILDS

Self-build is an option for earthships but the same impediments are in place as for major developments. Land costs are generally high as a proportion of the overall cost, construction costs relatively expensive and the labour involved is intensive. However, the individual may have more resilience to these factors than developers, particularly if they are committed to the principles at play in earthship construction. Self-build has been done extensively in New Mexico, but those builds have benefited enormously from large numbers of experienced earthship builders being available for advice, a large voluntary community available to help in the build and most importantly very cheap land. Both Earthship Brighton and Earthship Fife were built on land donated by the landowner or leased from a local authority with massive voluntary help and self-builds would almost certainly require similarly large voluntary workforces to be able to complete the build within a reasonable timescale. So if you have large numbers of generous friends who are unafraid of hard work you may be in luck; otherwise, it could be worth thinking twice about.

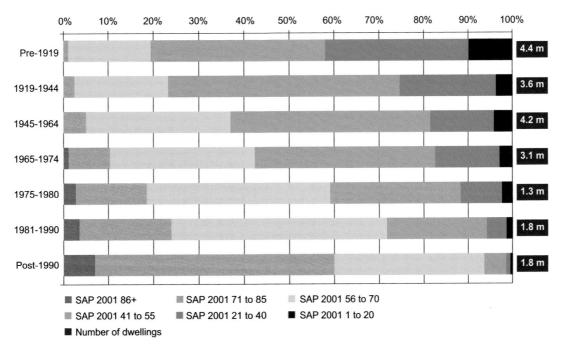

Figure 97: SAP ratings for dwellings from pre-1919 to post-1990 (based on the English House Condition Survey, 2004)

RETROFITTING THE EXISTING BUILDING STOCK

New build is, of course, only a small part of the carbon and sustainability problem in the UK, with the greater part of residential emissions derived from the existing building stock. And the government estimates that around 70% of the housing stock that will be standing in 2050 has already been built. This is problematic when even the most modern homes are relatively inefficient in terms of what is needed to become zero carbon. Despite the improvements represented by the 1990 implemented Part L of the Building Regulations, less than 10% of homes built after 1990 achieve a SAP rating of higher than 86, and the overall average residential SAP rating was 52 in 2004 compared to that in an exemplar development such as BedZED that has an effective SAP rating of 150.[8.10]

According to the Department of Communities and Local Government if all properties were improved by 10 SAP points, 4.5 MtC would be saved per annum. It also notes that it is through improvements made at the lower end of the SAP scale where energy performance is worst that relatively larger carbon savings will be achieved than at higher SAP levels.[8.11] So it must be a priority to improve the performance of these least efficient homes in order to reduce carbon emissions, although no specific proposals have been put forward to date to implement this.

Earthships can provide an inspiration here as well in terms of techniques and strategies that can be retrofitted to existing homes for energy demand reduction, increased efficiency and microgenerative possibilities. They are also provocative from the point of view of other sustainability measures such as water efficiency and the lessons learned from earthships need to be applied not only to new build but to housing in general.

CONCLUSION – TOWARD 2016

As the stated target from a number of senior government figures for achieving the zero carbon building milestone, 2016 deserves to stand as a major goal for the architectural and construction industry in the UK. Can it deliver on trying to slow down climate change and lay the foundations for a sustainable engagement with the planet rather than the crash course it has been on up to this point? That depends more than anything on political will to provide a framework of regulation and fiscal incentives that will encourage zero carbon development on a mass scale. At this stage there are no easy answers as to whether significant momentum will be achieved in the construction industry towards zero carbon: despite all the extremely positive talk there remains a paucity of the required meaningful action on the ground.

The momentum that is needed is not just about solving a statistical problem based on achieving zero carbon but about realising the fundamental requirement for paradigmatic change on all levels to try not to conquer or tame nature but to harness it positively and realise the necessary human connection with the natural environment. High carbon emissions are just one symptom of a failure to integrate buildings effectively with natural systems and the design of new buildings should surely be aiming not just to reduce carbon outputs but to have a more holistic engagement with sustainability in general. The earthship is emblematic of the type of change required in attitudes towards design and it eloquently showcases the way in which man can gain from his environment all the fundamental resources necessary for domestic life, in a sustainable and benign way. That is a valuable lesson in itself that all designers, developers, planners and self-builders can learn from, as well as those involved in other forms of ecologically destructive activities. And in this sense earthships will still be a guiding influence in 2016, serving as a pioneer example of the need to change the way in which we build homes.

Most predictions would suggest that the symptoms of climate change will become increasingly manifest in the coming years so that by 2016 there may be a significant amplification of many of the negative problems that are already occurring. Of course there is a requirement for global action as well as that in the UK, but the onus on developers here is clear:

there is now a moral obligation to act responsibly in terms of building impacts on the environment. Mankind's role is surely that of guardians of nature rather than owners of it. Building has always had a responsibility of legacy; that responsibility is now of the gravest kind – it has a significant role to play in protecting the very nature of the planet on which we live both for our own generation and for the generations yet to come.

REFERENCES AND NOTES

[8.1] AJ Specification (August 2006). Specifier's choice/Earthship Brighton.

[8.2] Building Design Magazine (January 19. 2007). Zero carbon should mean zero carbon, p15.

[8.3] See www.bbc.co.uk/climate/impact/flooding.shtml.

[8.4] Department of Communities and Local Government (2006). Building a greener future: Towards zero carbon development. Consultation document.

[8.5] Barker K (2004). Delivering stability: securing our future housing needs. Barker review of housing supply – final report – recommendations. London, HMSO.

[8.6] DCLG (2006). The code for sustainable homes.

[8.7] RIBA press release – www.riba.org/go/RIBA/News/Press_5910.html. Riddlestone – BioRegional (interview with author December 2006, both quotes published in Building for a Future magazine, winter edition 2007.

[8.8] Personal communication. E-mail from Mike Reynolds to the Mischa Hewitt.

[8.9] See the Biotecture website www.earthship.co.uk.

[8.10] Dunster B (2006). From A to ZED: Realising Zero (fossil) Energy Developments, (2nd ed). Wallington, Surrey, ZED Factory Ltd.

[8.11] DCLG (2006). The energy efficiency of homes – initial analysis.

REFERENCES AND NOTES

Chapter 1

[1.1] Stern N (2006). The economics of climate change: The Stern review. Executive summary (short). www.hm-treasury.gov.uk/media/999/76/CLOSED_SHORT_executive_summary.pdf.

[1.2] www.communities.gov.uk/index.asp?id=1002882&PressNoticeID=2320.

[1.3] EC Directive on the Energy Performance of Buildings (2002/91/EC of 16.12.2002).

[1.4] www.metoffice.gov.uk/corporate/pressoffice/2006/pr20060801.html.

[1.5] www.energywatch.org.uk/help_and_advice/energysmart/index.asp.

[1.6] Architects' Journal (8 July 1999).

[1.7] The BBC reported that the death toll had reached 220 000 on January 20, 2005. http://news.bbc.co.uk/1/hi/world/asia-pacific/4189883.stm.

[1.8] www.newscientist.com/article.ns?id=dn4259.

[1.9] www.nea.org.uk/Policy_&_Research/Fuel_poverty_facts/Excess_winter_mortality. The figures are taken from: Healy, JD, 2003. Excess winter mortality in Europe: a cross country analysis identifying key risk factors. Journal of Epidemiology and Community Health, volume 57, number 10.

[1.10] George Monbiot was talking at the Conway Hall on October 4, 2006 at an event organised by the Campaign Against Climate Change.

[1.11] www.royalsoc.ac.uk/landing.asp?id=1278.

[1.12] DEFRA (2006). UK climate change programme.

[1.13] Architects' Journal (19 June 2003). Earth mover (a profile of Mike Reynolds) by Kevin Telfer, pp18–19.

[1.14] www.metoffice.gov.uk/corporate/library/factsheets/factsheet14.pdf (p11). For New Mexico precipitation, see www.taosproperties.com/info.html.

The New Mexico figure is also based on anecdotal reports from Mike Reynolds and other Taos residents.

[1.15] Mike Reynolds' presentation to Green Party councillors at Brighton Town Hall on June 26, 2006.

[1.16] Le Corbusier is originally supposed to have said: 'Vous savez, c'est la vie qui a raison, l'architecte qui a tort'. He is quoted in Philippe Boudon, Lived-in architecture: Pessac Revisited, 1969. Translated by Gerald Onn. The statement is said to have been Le Corbusier's reply upon learning that the housing project he had designed at Pessac had been altered by its inhabitants.

[1.17] Stewart Baseley quoted in a Home Builders Federation press release on December 13, 2006. www.hbf.co.uk (news archive).

[1.18] Office of the Deputy Prime Minister (ODPM) 2006. Statistical release 2006/0042. "The number of households in England is projected to increase from 20.9 million in 2003 to 25.7 million by 2026, an annual growth of 209 000".

[1.19] Department of Communities and Local Government (DCLG) (2006). The energy efficiency of dwellings – initial analysis. p9.

[1.20] DTI (2003). Energy white paper: Our energy future – creating a low carbon economy. London, The Stationery Office.

Box 3 references and notes

[B1] DCLG (13 December 2006). News release: Towards a zero carbon future. www.communities.gov.uk/index.asp?id=1002882&PressNoticeID=2320.

[B2] BioRegional's response to UK government's announcements on zero carbon homes, 20 December 2006 www.bioregional.com/news%20page/news_stories/ZED/zerocarbon%20201206.htm.

[B3] Dunster B (2006). From A to ZED: Realising zero (fossil) energy developments, (2nd ed). Wallington, Surrey, ZED Factory Ltd.

Chapter 2

[2.1] See, for instance, the strapline of the article about Mike Reynolds in the Architects' Journal, 19 June 2003, p18: The earthships have landed – not aliens from another planet, but self-contained, environmentally friendly dwellings that their creator says points to the future.

[2.2] Boyle G (ed.) (2004). Renewable energy. Oxford, Oxford University Press.

[2.3] Desai P, King P (2006). One planet living: a guide to enjoying life on our one planet. Bristol, Alastair Sawday Publishing Co. Ltd.

[2.4] As reported by the BBC, see http://news.bbc.co.uk/1/hi/business/5101434.stm.

[2.5] Reynolds M (1990). Earthship volume 2: Systems and components. Taos, New Mexico, Solar Survival Press.

[2.6] Wines J (2000). Green architecture: The art of architecture in the age of ecology. London, Taschen.

[2.7] Telfer K (19 June 2003). Architects' Journal. Earth mover (a profile of Mike Reynolds), pp18 – 19.

[2.8] Report of the United Nations conference on environment and development (Rio de Janeiro, 3 to 14 June 1992). Principle 3 states "The right to development must be fulfilled so as to equitably meet developmental and environmental needs of present and future generations." See www.un.org/documents/ga/conf151/aconf15126-1annex1.htm).

[2.9] For ZED standard see: Dunster, B 2006. From A to ZED: Realising zero (fossil) energy developments. Second edition. Wallington, Surrey; ZED Factory Ltd. For Passivhaus see www.passivhaus.org.uk/index.jsp?id=668. For the work of Brenda and Robert Vale see The new autonomous house, Thames and Hudson, 2000. For One planet living see reference [2.3] For AECB see www.aecb.net.

[2.10] DCLG (2006). The energy efficiency of homes – initial analysis p1.

[2.11] DCLG statistical release 2006/0042: "The number of households in England is projected to increase from 20.9 million in 2003 to 25.7 million by 2026, an annual growth of 209,000".

[2.12] For used tyre statistics see: www.wrap.org.uk/construction/tyres/dti_used_tyre_statistics/index.html.

Box 4 references and notes

[B1] Shukman H (19 March 2006). New age New Mexico. The Observer.

[B2] Telfer K (19 June 2003). Earth mover (a profile of Mike Reynolds). Architects' Journal, pp18 to 19.

[B3] Email from Mike Reynolds to Kevin Telfer, January, 2007.

Chapter 3

[3.1] Carbon Trust (2006). The carbon emissions generated in all that we consume.

[3.2] ArupGeotechnics (2002). Ground storage of building heat energy: overview report O-02-ARUP3, DTI Partners in Innovation.

Chapter 4

[4.1] R Buckminster Fuller (1976). Operating manual for spaceship earth. New York, Aenonian Press.

[4.2] DTI (2003). Energy white paper.

[4.3] DCLG (2006). Energy review.

[4.4] DCLG (2006) The code for sustainable homes.

[4.5] Dunster B (2006). From A to ZED: Realising zero (fossil) energy developments. (2nd ed). Wallington, Surrey, ZED Factory Ltd.

[4.6] Sustainable Consumption Roundtable (2005). Seeing the light: the impact of microgeneration on the way we use energy – qualitative research findings. Written and researched by The Hub Research Consultants on behalf of the Sustainable Consumption Roundtable.Download from www.sd-commission.org.uk.

[4.7] LCCA. Presentation by Allan Jones, chief executive officer, London Climate Change Agency: Urban change on a large-scale at: Renewable energy in the new low carbon Britain: 2020 and beyond. A conference hosted by the Energy Institute, 5 December 2006.

[4.8] Poyry Consulting. Presentation by Richard Slark: The role of renewables in the UK generation mix: independent forecasts for 2010, 2015 and 2020 at Renewable energy in the new low carbon

Britain: 2020 and beyond. A conference hosted by the Energy Institute, 5 December 2006.

[4.9] NPower. Presentation by Robert Harper, product manager. Environment and renewables: NPower proceedings at Renewable energy in the new low carbon Britain: 2020 and beyond. A conference hosted by the Energy Institute, 5 December 2006.

[4.10] Renewable Energy Association. Presentation by Philip Wolfe, chief executive officer at Renewable energy in the new low carbon Britain: 2020 and beyond. A conference hosted by the Energy Institute, 5 December 2006.

[4.11] See the BBC website, for example, which offers numerous tips on saving energy in the home: http://news.bbc.co.uk/1/hi/uk/6076658.stm.

[4.12] Boyle G (ed) (2004). Renewable energy. Oxford, Oxford University Press, p31.

[4.13] Reynolds M (1990). Earthship Volume 1: How to build your own. Taos, New Mexico, Solar Survival Press.

[4.14] ODPM (2005). ODPM statistical release 2006/0042.

[4.15] Reynolds M (2006). A presentation to Green Party councillors at Brighton Town Hall on June 26, 2006; also conversations with the authors.

[4.16] DCLG (2004). Planning Policy Statement 22: Renewable energy.

Chapter 5

[5.1] See www.metoffice.gov.uk/climate/uk/location/england.

[5.2] See www.environment agency.gov.uk/regions/midlands.

[5.3] See www.defra.gov.uk/corporate/ministers/statements/em060301.htm.

[5.4] See www.environment-agency.gov.uk.

[5.5] See www.ofwat.gov.uk/aptrix/ofwat/publish.nsf/Content/navigation-ofwat-faqs-statistics.

[5.6] See www.ofwat.gov.uk/aptrix/ofwat/publish.nsf/Content/customers_in_eng_wales.

[5.7] Stauffer J (1996). Safe to drink? The quality of your water. Machynnlleth, Centre of Alternative Technology Publications.

[5.8] See www.ofwat.gov.uk.

[5.9] See www.waterwise.org.uk.

[5.10] Watkins (2006). Human Development Report 2006: Beyond scarcity: Power, poverty and the global water crisis. New York, United Nations Development Programme.

[5.11] See www.communities.gov.uk/index.asp?id=1002882&PressNoticeID=2097.

[5.12] ech2o are environmental consultants offering design advice and seminars on all aspects of sustainable water use, low or zero carbon energy systems, carbon literacy and environmental choice of materials. See www.ech2o.co.uk.

[5.13] See www.ukhra.org.

[5.14] See www.metoffice.gov.uk/climate/uk/averages/19712000/index.html.

[5.15] Reynolds M (2005). Water from the sky. Taos, New Mexico, Solar Survival Press.

[5.16] Parsloe C (2005). CIBSE knowledge series: reclaimed water. London, The Chartered Institute of Building Services Engineers (CIBSE).

[5.17] Leggett D J, Brown R, Brewer D and Holliday E (2001). Rainwater and greywater use in buildings: Decision making for water conservation. London, CIRIA.

[5.18] Cowie P (2004). The earthship toolkit: Your guide to building a zero waste zero energy future. Kinghorn, Sustainable Communities Initiatives.

Chapter 6

[6.1] WRAP – for used tyre statistics see: www.wrap.org.uk/construction/tyres/dti_used_tyre_statistics/index.html.

[6.2] Reynolds M (1990). Earthship Volume 1: How to build your own. Taos, New Mexico, Solar Survival Press, p77.

[6.3] Reynolds M (1990). Earthship Volume 1: How to build your own. Taos, New Mexico, Solar Survival Press, p78.

[6.4] WRAP statement (2006). Press office statement to the author, Kevin Telfer.

[6.5] For details of the Landfill Tax Credit Scheme and its objects see: www.ltcs.org.uk.

[6.6] The Guardian (November 19, 2006). 'Smart' homes to eat their rubbish.

[6.7] www.britglass.org.uk/Education/Recycling.html.

[6.8] Architects' Journal (19 June 2003). Earth mover (a profile of Mike Reynolds) by Kevin Telfer, pp18 – 19.

[6.9] BRE (2006). Domestic energy factfile. Download from http://projects.bre.co.uk/factfile/TenureFactFile2006.pdf.

[6.10] AJ Specification (August 2006). Specifier's choice/Earthship Brighton.

[6.11] Environment Council (2004). Required exemptions to waste management licensing for tyre recovery.

[6.12] Mike Reynolds M (1990). Earthship Volume 2: Systems and components. Taos, New Mexico, Solar Survival Press.

[6.13] www.woodrecycling.org.uk.

Chapter 7

[7.1] Reynolds M (1990). Earthship volume 1: How to build your own. Taos, New Mexico, Solar Survival Press, pp44-46.

[7.2] See the Gaia research report on www.gaiagroup.org for a detailed analysis of the risks to tyres.

[7.3] www.guardian.co.uk/wastestory/0,12188,747921,00.html.

[7.4] Reynolds, M (2001). Comfort in any climate. Taos, New Mexico, Solar Survival Press.

[7.5] Cowie P (2004). The earthship toolkit: Your guide to building a zero waste zero energy future. Kinghorn, Sustainable Communities Initiatives.

[7.6] BRE (2007). U-value calculator. Available from www.brebookshop.com.

[7.7] BuildDesk U version 3.2. www.builddesk.co.uk/graphics/BuildDesk_UK/ OUR_SOFTWARE/ BuildDesk_U/2_BD-data_U-UK.pdf.

Chapter 8

[8.1] AJ Specification (August 2006). Specifier's choice/Earthship Brighton.

[8.2] Building Design Magazine (January 19. 2007). Zero carbon should mean zero carbon, p15.

[8.3] See www.bbc.co.uk/climate/impact/flooding.shtml.

[8.4] Department of Communities and Local Government (2006). Building a greener future: Towards zero carbon development. Consultation document.

[8.5] Barker K (2004).Delivering stability: securing our future housing needs. Barker review of housing supply – final report – recommendations. London, HMSO.

[8.6] DCLG (2006). The code for sustainable homes.

[8.7] RIBA press release - www.riba.org/go/RIBA/News/Press_5910.html. Riddlestone – BioRegional (interview with author December 2006, both quotes published in Building for a Future magazine, winter edition 2007.

[8.8] Personal communication. e-mail from Mike Reynolds to the Mischa Hewitt.

[8.9] See the Biotecture website www.earthship.co.uk.

[8.10] Dunster B (2006). From A to ZED: Realising Zero (fossil) Energy Developments, (2nd ed). Wallington, Surrey, ZED Factory Ltd.

[8.11] DCLG (2006). The energy efficiency of homes – initial analysis.

RECOMMENDED READING

Benyus J (2002). Biomimicry: Innovation inspired by nature. New York, Harper Perennial. ISBN: 0060533226.

Boyle G (2003). Energy systems and sustainability. Oxford, Oxford University Press. ISBN: 0199261792.

Butti K, Perlin J (1980). Golden thread: Twenty five hundred years of solar architecture and technology. Frodsham, Cheshire Books. ISBN: 0917352076.

Campbell S (1984). Home water supply: How to find, filter and conserve it. North Adams, Storey Books. ISBN: 0882663240.

Campbell C (1997). The coming oil crisis. Brentwood, Multi Science Publishing Co Ltd. ISBN: 0906522110.

Day C (2006). Places of the soul: Architecture and environmental design as a healing art. Oxford, Architectural Press. ISBN: 0750659017.

Desai P, Riddlestone S (2002). Schumacher briefings 8: Bioregional solutions – for living on one planet. Dartington, Green Books. ISBN: 1903998077.

Douthwaite R (1999). Schumacher briefings 4: The ecology of money. Dartington, Green Books. ISBN: 1870098811.

Ehrlich P (1971). Population bomb. New York, Buccaneer Books. ISBN: 1568495870.

Elliot D (2003). Schumacher briefings 10: A solar world – climate change and the green energy revolution. Dartington, Green Books. ISBN: 190399831X.

Environment Agency (1998). Tyres in the environment. Environmental issue series. ISBN: 1873160755.

Gipe P (1999). Wind energy basics: A guide to small and micro wind systems. White River Junction, Chelsea Green Publishing Company. ISBN: 1890132071.

Giradet H (1999). Schumacher briefings 2: Creating sustainable cities. Dartington, Green Books. ISBN: 1870098773.

Girling R (2005). Rubbish: Dirt on our hands and crisis ahead. London, Transworld. ISBN: 1903919444.

Heinberg R (2004). Powerdown: Options and actions for a post-carbon world (2nd ed). Clairview Books. ISBN: 1902636635.

Heinberg R (2005). Party's over: Oil, war and the fate of industrial societies. (2nd ed). Clairview Books. ISBN: 1905570007.

Kachadorian J (1997). The passive solar house: Using solar design to heat and cool your home. White River Junction, Chelsea Green Publishing Company. ISBN: 0930031970.

Leggett J (2006). Half gone: Oil, gas, hot air, and the global energy crisis. London, Portobello Books. ISBN: 1846270057.

Mazria E (1979). Passive solar energy book. New York, Rodale Publishing. ISBN: 0878572376

Lovelock J (2000). Gaia: A new look at life on earth. Oxford, Oxford University Press. ISBN: 0192862189.

Lovelock J (2006). The revenge of Gaia. London, Penguin Books Ltd. ISBN: 0713999144.

Lynas M (2007). Carbon calculator: Easy ways to reduce you carbon footprint. London, Harper Collins Publishers. ISBN: 9780007258697.

Meadows DH (2004). The limits to growth: The 30-year update. London, Earthscan Publications Ltd. ISBN: 1844071448.

Mobbs P (2005). Energy beyond oil. Leicester, Matador Publishing. ISBN: 1905237006.

Monbiot G (2006). Heat - How to stop the planet from burning. London, Penguin Books Ltd. ISBN: 0713999233.

Porrit J (2005). Capitalism: As if the world matters. London, Earthscan Publications Ltd. ISBN: 1844071928.

Roaf S, Crichton D, Nicoll F (2005). Adapting buildings and cities for climate change: A 21st century survival guide. Oxford, Architectural Press. ISBN: 0750659114.

Roaf S, Fuentes M, Thomas, S (2007). Ecohouse 2: A design guide. (2nd ed). Oxford, Architectural Press. ISBN: 0750657340.

Scheer H (2004). The solar economy: Renewable energy for a sustainable global future. London, Earthscan Publications Ltd. ISBN: 1844070751.

Schumacher E (1993). Small is beautiful: a study of economics as if people mattered. London, Vintage. ISBN: 0099225611.

Scott N (2005). Reduce, reuse, recycle: An easy household guide. Dartington, Green Books. ISBN: 1903998409.

Simmons M (2005). Twilight in the desert: The coming Saudi oil shock and the world economy. Chichester, John Wiley & Sons. ISBN: 047173876X.

Wolverton B (1996). Eco friendly house plants. London, George Weidenfeld & Nicolson Ltd. ISBN: 0297834843.

INDEX

Page number in *italics* refer to illustrations.

A

adobe, wall finishing *24*, 97
aesthetics, earthships 21–2, 88
aluminium cans, as building material *84*, 86–7, 97
Association for Environment Conscious Building (AECB) 25

B

Barker review 57, 112
BedZED 31, 47–8, *47*, 113, 116
bioenergy 53
BioRegional 12
blackwater, treatment of *27*, 64–5, 73–4, *74*
bottle walls *5*, *18*, *83*, 86, 87, *87*, 100–1
BowZED *111*
Brighton, 'The Lizard' development 114–15
Brighton Earthship *see* Earthship Brighton
Brighton and Hove Wood Recycling Project 88
building materials
    low impact 25–8
    recycled 19–20, 25–6, 77, 100
see also tyres
buildings, existing 116
Butler, Trevor 112

C

cans, aluminium *84*, 86–7, 97

carbon footprint
    housing 31, 116
    see also zero carbon housing
chemicals, for cleaning 72–3
climate change, effects of 2–8, 110
Code for Sustainable Homes 2, 9–10, 25, 47, 110, 112
Craigencalt Ecology Centre 101

D

Department for Communities and Local Government (DCLG) 2, 12, 25
Dunster, Bill 48

E

earth, use in tyre construction 80, *80*, 92
Earthship Brighton
    blackwater treatment 73
    as case study 11
    conservatory 34, *87*, *90*
    energy supply *45*, 50, 51, *52*, *53*, 56
    excavation of site 91–2, *91*
    floor construction *34*, 97
    glass bottle walls *86*
    glazing 35
    greywater system 70, *71*, 72, 99
    microgeneration *45*
    passive solar design 32, *33*
    plan *36*
    project overview 102–4
    roof construction 66, 96, 97, 99
    septic tank *72*, 73

solar thermal power *45*, *53*, *54*
thermal evaluation report 36–42
thermal mass 33–5
thermal wrap *32*, 94
timber frame 98, *98*
timeline 103
ventilation 99–100, *100*
wall construction *26*, 92–4, *93*, *94*, 96
wall packout 97, *97*
waste management regulations 82–4, 89
water collection 66–7, *67*, 68
water system 69, 72, 73, 99
wind turbine *45*, *52*, 53
wood pellet stove 55, *55*
Earthship Fife
    blackwater treatment *27*, 73–4, *74*
    energy supply 56
    greywater system *28*, 71, 72
    microhydro 55
    passive solar design 32
    project overview 102–104
    roof 66
    thermal mass 35
    Turgo Runner Stram Engine microhydro turbine 55
    visitor centre *20*, *101*
    waste management regulations 82
    water collection 66, 68
earthships
    aesthetics and functionality 21–2
    building materials 25–8
    definition 15
    design developments 20, 24

energy strategy 51
future of 107, 114–15
insulation 34, *34*
as mass housing 113–14
origins of 8–9, 19–20
passive solar design 26–7,
32–3
perception of 113
renewable energy 27, 45–6
roof materials 66
self-builds 115
self-sufficiency 16, 18–19
site harmony 16–18, 108
site selection 91–2
stacked 113
sustainability 24–5
thermal mass 33–4, 81,
109–10
in the UK 9–11
water supply 27–8
water systems 65–74, 99, 110
eco-cement 97, *98*
eco-psychology 22
Eden Project
photovoltaic panels *54*
rainwater harvesting *60*
electricity
national grid 49–51
see *also* energy
energy
bioenergy 53
climate change impacts 2–4
costs 3, 55–7
earthships 51
microgeneration *45*, 48, 52–5
microhydro 55, *55*
photovoltaic 53
renewable 27, 45–58
solar 51–2
solar thermal power 53, *53*,
54
wind power *45*, 52–3, *52*, *53*
Energy Performance of Buildings
Directive 2
Energy review (2006) 46, 57
Energy white paper (2003) 46–7,
57

Environment Agency
waste management
regulations 82–4, 89
water resources 61–2
European Union, Landfill
Directive 82

F

Fife Earthship see *Earthship Fife*
Findhorn eco-village 47
floor
construction 97
insulation 34, *34*
food production 28, 73, 114
foundations 97
functionality, earthships 21–2

G

glass bottles, as building material
5, *18*, *83*, *86*, *87*, *87*, 100–1
greenhouse gases 6
greywater, recycling 28, 64,
69–73, *70*, *71*

H

heating
solar 51–2, 109–10
see *also* temperature
Hockerton Housing Project 25,
31, 47, 113
blackwater treatment 64–5,
65
Hyett, Paul 3

I

infrastructure
critique of 108–9
electricity 49–51
water 62–3
Institute for Public Policy
Research (IPPR) 79
insulation, earthships 34, *34*
Intergovernmental Panel on
Climate Change (IPCC) 6–7

J

'junk aesthetic' 88

K

King, David 79
Kinghorn Loch see *Earthship Fife*

L

Landfill Tax Credit Scheme (LTCS)
79
London Climate Change Agency
(LCCA) 48
Low Carbon Network Ltd (LCN)
82–3, 102
Low Carbon Trust 79, 104
Lyall, Sutherland 81, 110

M

microgeneration
bioenergy 53
cost implications 55–7
energy supply 48, 52
future of 58
microhydro 55
photovoltaics *45*, 53
solar thermal power *45*,
53–54, *53*
wind power *45*, 52–3, *52*, *53*
microhydro 55, *55*
Monbiot, George 5

N

natural disasters, architecture and
4–5
natural resources, use of 18
New Mexico see *Taos, New
Mexico*
New Orleans, flooding 4

O

'one planet living' 18, 25, 108

P

passive solar design 26–7,
   32–3, *33*, 51–2, 109–10
Passivhaus system 25
Pearce, Nick 79
Phoenix earthship *see* New
   Mexico
photovoltaic power 53
planters
   choice of plants 73
   construction of 99
   greywater treatment 28, *28*,
      69–73, *70*, *71*
power supply *see* energy
Pringle, Jack 112

R

rainwater, harvesting 27–8,
   63–4, 66–8, *67*, 110
Randall, Martin 115
recycled materials
   for building 19–20, 25–6, *77*,
      86–9, 100, 109
   see also waste materials
Reynolds, Mike
   biography 23
   on building materials 22
   earthship origins 8, 9, 19
   on energy supply 52, 55
   on future developments 114
   on water recycling 64
Riddlestone, Sue 112
risk assessment, tyres 85
roof construction, earthships 66,
   96

S

SAP energy ratings 116
Scottish Environmental Protection
   Agency (SEPA) 82
self-builds, earthships 115
self-sufficiency, earthships 16,
   18–19
septic tank 70, 72, *72*, 73, 99

sewage, blackwater treatment *27*,
   64–5, 73–4, *74*
site
   harmony 16–18, 108
   suitable 91–2
solar energy
   passive solar design 26–7,
      32–3, 51–2, 109–10
   solar thermal power 51, 53,
      53, *54*
Stern review 2, 110
stone, use of offcuts *87*, 88
sun
   orientation towards 17, 32
   use of 18
   see also solar energy
sustainability
   earthships 24–5
   UK housing 9–11

T

Taos, New Mexico
   earthships 8, 17, 65
   Estrada earthship *9*, *22*
   food production 28
   hybrid earthship *1*, *15*
   Jacobsen earthship *10*, *83*
   kitchens *4*, *9*
   Kurnizi earthship *24*
   Phoenix earthship 28, 73, 114
   split-level earthship *17*
temperature
   global rise 6–7
   regulation 33–5
   see also heating
thermal mass 33–4, 81, 109–10
thermal performance, Earthship
   Brighton 36–42
thermal wrap *32*, 33–4, *94*
timber, recycled 88
timber frame 98
toilets
   compost toilets 65
   flushing system 28, 64, *72*, 73
   use of chemicals 72–3
   see also blackwater
tsunami (2004) 4

Turgo Runner Stream Engine
   microhydro turbine *55*
tyres
   as building material 19–20,
      25–6, 77–81, *78*, *79*, 109
   construction method 80, 92,
      93, *94*
   landfill *77*, *77*
   ramming with earth 80, *80*,
      92
   regulations 82–6, 89
   risk assessment 85
   sizing 95
   suitability 95

U

United Kingdom
   energy resources 46–8
   future earthships 114–15
   sustainable housing 9–11, 25
   water resources 61–3
   zero carbon housing 110–13

V

Vale, Robert and Brenda 25, 47
ventilation 99–100, *100*

W

walls
   bottle walls *5*, *18*, *83*, *86*, *87*,
      87, 100–1
   packed out 97, *97*
   see also tyres
waste materials
   regulations 82–4, 85–6, 89
   see also recycled materials
Waste and Resources Action
   Programme (WRAP) 79, 82
water
   blackwater *27*, 64–5, 73–4,
      74
   earthship system 65–74, 99,
      110
   greywater 28, 64, 69–73, *70*,
      71
   potable 67–69

rainwater harvesting 27–8,
  63–4, 66–8
recycling 64–5
self-sufficiency 19, 27–8
storage 66–8, *67*
UK resources 61–4
waste treatment 28
wind power, microgeneration
  45, 52–3, *52*, *53*
Wines, James 21, 22

Z

ZED Factory 12, 48
ZED standard 25
  see also BedZED
zero carbon housing
  definitions 12, 58
  earthships as solution 113–14
  future 116–17
  government targets 2, 9–11,
25, 47, 108, 110–13